JAILED
FOR PEACE

The History of
American Draft
Law Violators,
1658–1985

Stephen M. Kohn

PRAEGER

New York
Westport, Connecticut
London

Library of Congress Cataloging-in-Publication Data

Kohn, Stephen M. (Stephen Martin)
  Jailed for peace.

  Bibliography: p.
  Includes index.
  1. Conscientious objectors—United States—History.
2. Military service, Compulsory—United States—Draft
resisters.   3. Conscientious objectors—Legal status,
laws, etc.—United States—History.   I. Title.
UB343.K64   1987   355.2′24′0973   87-10359
ISBN 0-275-92776-8 (pbk. : alk. paper)

A hardcover edition of *Jailed for Peace: The History of American Draft
Law Violators, 1658-1985* is available from Greenwood Press (Contributions
in Military Studies; 49; ISBN 0-313-24586-X).

Library of Congress Catalog Number: 87-10359
ISBN: 0-275-92776-8

First published 1986

Paperback edition 1987

Praeger Publishers, One Madison Avenue, New York, NY 10010
A division of Greenwood Press, Inc.

Printed in the United States of America

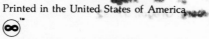

The paper used in this book complies with the Permanent
Paper Standard issued by the National
Information Standards Organization (Z39.48-1984).

10 9 8 7 6 5 4 3 2 1

To my brother, Michael

Contents

Tables

Acknowledgments

This book was made possible, in part, by a Youthgrant from the National Endowment for the Humanities, the support of the Northeastern University School of Law, and my family, Corinne, Arthur, Margaretta, Michael, and Estelle. I would also like to thank the following people and organizations for their assistance: David Koff, Connie McKenna, Heather Horak, Judy Somberg, Paul Hendrie, residents of 1611 Hobart Street, Frederick Brown, New Travel, Paul Bowan, Elmer Cornwell, Michael Meltsner, Howard Zinn, Sam Doud, Gene Sharpe, Debbie Smith, the Government Accountability Project, Rita Simmons, Mark Toney, Jenny Patchen, Mari Jo Buhle, Roger Nash Baldwin, the Central Committee for Conscientious Objectors, Ralph DiGia, J. F. Libertelli, Paul Peloquin, Judy Linsky, Jeremy Firestone, Glen Marcus, Ramsey Clark, the Rhode Island Coalition Against Registration and the Draft, Jerry Elmer, the New England American Friends Service Committee, the War Resisters League, the Rhode Island American Friends Service Committee, Ray Rickman, Charles Maresca, L. William Yolton, the Brown University Political Science Department, Ron Martin-Adkins, and the National Interreligious Service Board for Conscientious Objectors.

For their excellent collections which contained information on conscientious objectors, I am indebted to the following libraries: the Princeton University American Civil Liberties Union Collection, the Swarthmore College Peace Collection, the National Archives and Records Service, the Brandeis University ACLU Micro-film Collection, and the Boston Public Library collection on abolitionist literature.

For the use of their materials, I would also like to thank the following libraries: Northeastern University Dodge Library, Northeastern University Law Library, Antioch School of Law Library, Stockton State College Library, Brown University Rockefeller Library, Brown University John Hay Library, and Providence Public Library.

JAILED
FOR PEACE

Introduction

In the winter of 1918 a young draft resister in a Fort Andrews stockade was kicked and severely beaten by his guards. The guards placed a rope around his neck and hung him from the rafters until he nearly suffocated. Fortunately, his life was spared, although seventeen of his comrades would die from neglect and abuse in military jails. The First World War was popular; his pacifist cause was not. Yet even while his hands were swollen from continuous beatings, the resister wrote defiantly from jail: "My willpower is stronger than the bayonet and my ideas will not be shot out of my head."[1]

From earliest colonial days, when American conscientious objectors refused to fight against Native American tribes, until the early 1980s when 500,000 youths refused to register for the draft, Americans have consistently violated conscription laws. Draft resistance is one of the largest, longest, and most successful campaigns of civil disobedience in American history. Resisters have contributed to altering American foreign and military policy, pioneering direct action tactics, and developing pacifist and humanistic ideals. Resisters have made significant and lasting contributions to civil and religious liberty. They have been a powerful, catalytic force in the modern peace movement.

Despite their important contributions to American history and social change, no book has been published which fully documents the history and political impact of anti-war conscientious objectors. This book was written to fill that unfortunate void.

NOTE

1. Philip Grosser, Letters from Prison, February 24, 1918, and February 28, 1918, ACLU, 1918.

1

Colonial Roots

The roots of the modern anti-draft movement are buried deep within the early American colonial experience. Although the New World was stained with blood from innumerable battles—battles between competing European powers, battles between colonists and Indians, and battles over religious toleration—it was not warriors alone who carved out the New World in America. Peacemakers also settled America. These settlers refused to appropriate land from or fight with the Indians. Many would not own slaves. And, when called into military service for the King, they refused to be conscripted. They did not fight for peace, but they stood quietly against war.[1]

There are numerous stories of settlers who, in the face of great risk, would not arm themselves against the Indians. One incident occurred on the frontier of western New York and Pennsylvania in the early 1600s. During a period of "Indian hostilities," local authorities urged a community of Quakers to enter the local army fort. Considering this a retreat behind arms, the Quakers maintained their religious commitment to nonviolence by continuing their normal activities:

One day while sitting in silent devotion in their rude meeting house, a party of Indians suddenly approached the place, painted and armed for the work of slaughter. They passed to and fro by the open door of the house, looking inquisitively within and about the building, till having sufficiently reconnoitered the quiet worshippers, they at length respectfully entered and joined them. They were met by the principal Friends with the outstretched hand of peace, and shown to such seats as the house afforded, which they occupied in reverent silence till the meeting was regularly dissolved. They were then invited to one of the nearest dwellings by the leading man of the Society, and hospitably refreshed. On their departure the Indian chief took his host aside, and pledged him and his people perfect security from all depredations of the red men. Said he, "when Indian come to his place, Indian meant to tomahawk every white man he found. But Indian found white man with no guns, no fighting weapons, so still, so peaceable, worshiping Great Spirit, the Great Spirit say in the Indian's heart—no hurt them, no hurt them!"[2]

The first recorded instance of pacifist resistance to military conscription in America was in the province of Maryland in 1658. For "refusing to be trained as a solider," Richard Keene was fined and "abused by the sheriff, who drew his cutlass and therewith made a pass at the breast of the said Richard, and struck him on the shoulders, saying: 'You dog, I could find it in my heart to split your brains.' "[3] Pacifists were ill-treated in other colonies as well. For example, disgruntlement over Quaker friendship with "heathen" Indians led colonial officials to lambast the "monstrous" doctrine of pacifism. A militia law was passed requiring citizens to arm and train in order to fight Indians. The colonial records of the North Carolina colony reveal that "lazy" and "cowardly" Quaker pacifists were subject to "fines and penalties" for refusing to comply with this draft law.[4]

In response to militia laws, Quakers and pacifists engaged in "passive resistance," an early form of civil disobedience. The first occurrence of mass noncompliance to the draft took place in an area called West New Jersey in 1704. Quakers had purchased the deed to West New Jersey in 1676. They settled on the land, established a pacifist military policy, and wrote one of the first colonial charters to guarantee freedom of religion and conscience.[5] But in 1703, West New Jersey merged with East New Jersey, and an anti-Quaker governor was appointed. The following year, the governor passed a broad militia act that provided heavy fines and property confiscation for those people who refused military training. New Jersey residents condemned the law as an anti-Quaker measure, and local constables declined to enforce it. When the attorney general attempted to prosecute the rebellious constables, a sympathetic jury refused to convict. Within a year the Crown disallowed the law, and the legislature failed to reenact the measure. All subsequent colonial New Jersey militia laws contained liberal provisions that allowed Quakers to escape compulsory service.[6]

During the French and Indian War, the state of Virginia imprisoned a small group of Quakers for failing to cooperate with a 1756 Virginia militia law. This law required all young men to participate in a lottery and to draw draft lots. Seven Quakers refused to participate and were jailed. "After a week in jail," military correspondence reads, "they were brought before the court. . . . They asserted their readiness to comply with the law in all things not against their conscience. But, they said, 'to bear arms or fight we could not.' "[7] The objectors were taken to Colonel George Washington's headquarters. There, Governor Robert Dinwiddle of Virginia ordered Washington to confine the group in a stockade "with a short allowance of bread and water" until brought to "reason."[8] Washington, however, was moved by the courage and determination of the objectors. He wrote back to the Governor: "I could by no means bring the Quakers to any terms. They chose rather to be whipped to death than bear arms."[9] Washington ordered the seven objectors freed from the guardhouse and granted them permission to live with local Quakers until their militia obligations ended. Upon receiving thanks from the group, an account records that Washington "told them they were welcome, and all he asked of them in return was that if ever he should fall as much into their power as they had in his, they would treat him with equal kindness."[10]

THE RHODE ISLAND AND PENNSYLVANIA EXPERIMENTS

Pacifists were an oppressed minority in some colonies; in others, they constituted a majority or plurality of the population. In those colonies, pacifists were in the forefront of the establishment of important religious and civil liberties. Rhode Island offers an interesting case study in the challenges faced by a pacifist-dominated colony. In 1663, it became the first American colony to establish a fundamental right to religious liberty.[11] In its early days, the colonial government was Quaker. Instead of warring against the Indians, the government adopted an "enlightened and humane" policy and refused to sanction the exploitation of Native Americans.[12]

In 1673, fearing attack by both Dutch settlers and hostile Indians, the colonial government passed an emergency militia bill. But because it considered conscientious objection part of the fundamental law of "liberty of conscience," the legislature passed one of the New World's earliest conscientious objector (CO) exemptions. It proved to be the broadest exemption to active-duty combat in American history. The law exempted from active military duty all those who for reasons of conscience could not "train, arm, rally to fight, to kill."[13] The law read:

Noe person nor persons [within this colony], that is or hereafter shall be persuaded in his, their conscience, or consciences [and by him or them declared], that he nor they cannot nor ought not to trayne, to learned to fight, nor to war, nor kill any person or persons . . . nor shall suffer any punishment, fine, distraint, penalty nor imprisonment.[14]

When New England was torn by Indian wars in 1675–1677, the Rhode Island government condemned the war and refused to support the war effort of its neighboring colonies. The governments of these colonies dispatched an official complaint to King Charles II of England protesting Rhode Island's refusal to participate in the war.[15]

Pennsylvania colony was founded by the radical Quaker William Penn. Penn, along with hundreds of other Quakers, suffered persecution in England for his religious beliefs.[16] Penn intended to create a territory where freedom of conscience would be absolute and Quaker concepts of peace and social justice could be realized.[17] The *Pennsylvania Charter of Privilege* (1701), drafted by William Penn, is widely recognized as a milestone in the development of democratic rights.[18]

In one of his first actions as founder of Pennsylvania, Penn made peace with the native Indians, refrained from forming a militia, and established a series of civil rights unheard of in other colonies. These included the right to jury trial and the abolition of debtors' prison.[19] Penn believed in nonviolent means to establish liberty throughout the colony. As he wrote in a tract on Quakerism: "Not fighting, but suffering . . . affirm that Christianity teacheth people to beat their swords into ploughshares, and their spears into pruning hooks, and to learn war no more."[20]

Despite considerable pressure from the Crown, Pennsylvania refused to establish a militia until the outbreak of the French and Indian War. As early as 1689, the colonial legislature was rebuking calls from the Crown to form an army. One legislator denounced the formation of a military, stating: "I had rather be ruined than violate my conscience."[21] Later, in 1739, the royal governor pleaded with the legislature to establish a militia. Again the request was denied. Quaker legislators condemned the idea as a "direct breach of our charter."[22] In 1754, at the onset of the French and Indian War, the royal governor again presented the case for a militia to the Assembly. He proposed a militia bill exempting those "conscientious scrupulous of bearing arms." The Assembly compromised, establishing a strictly voluntary militia.[23] But the Assembly remained unequivocal about the rights of conscience. No person would be required to join the militia against his conscience, even if the very existence of the colony was at stake. As one colonial legislator put it: "We have taken every step in our power, consistent with the just rights of the freemen. . . . Those who would give up essential liberty to purchase a little temporary safety, deserve neither liberty nor safety."[24]

THE REVOLUTIONARY PERIOD

At the dawn of the American Revolution, the civil libertarian influences of Pennsylvania and Rhode Island together with the passive resistance of Quakers and pacifists in other colonies had a substantial impact. Every colony with a sizable pacifist population recognized conscientious objection as a valid ground for exemption from militia duty.[25] These colonies in-

cluded Massachusetts, New Hampshire, North Carolina, South
Carolina, Virginia, and New York.[26] One of the earliest laws
passed by the Continental Congress in 1775 was a statute exempting COs from military duty.[27]

The rights of conscience were protected even when the invasion of important cities by British troops seemed imminent.
A revealing letter to the Pennsylvania Council of Safety from
George Washington, Commander of the Revolutionary Army,
warned that the British were planning to attack Philadelphia
and called for the conscription of all persons, *except* conscientious objectors. Washington wrote, "As there is not the least
doubt at present, that the principal object of the enemy is to
get possession of the City of Philadelphia, it is absolutely necessary, that every person able to bear arms [except such as
are Conscientiously scrupulous against in every case] should
give their personal service."[28] Four revolutionary state governments proclaimed conscientious objection an absolute right
in their new constitutions. These states were Delaware (1776
Declaration of Rights, Sec. 40), Pennsylvania (1776 Declaration of Rights, Sec. 8), New York (1777 Constitution, Sec. 40),
and New Hampshire (1784 Constitution, Sec. 8).

Despite these protections, a small number of religious objectors suffered imprisonment and fines during the American
Revolution. One conscientious objector was imprisoned for two
years in Lancaster, Pennsylvania.[29] In another case, an objector from North Carolina was whipped for refusing induction
into the state militia: "Forty stripes were very heavily laid on,
by three different persons, with a whip having nine cords. . . .[30]
Overall, the majority of Revolutionary War objectors were exempted from military service, and those who were jailed only
served very short sentences [one or two days]."[31]

After the Revolution, there was widespread support for in-
corporating a conscientious objector exemption into the Bill of
Rights. When the newly drafted U.S. Constitution was de-
bated in the state ratification conventions, four states passed
resolutions or minority reports calling for a constitutional
amendment protecting conscientious objectors.[32] James Madison, while a representative in the House of Representatives
during the First Congress, introduced the Bill of Rights into

the House. He included an exemption from state militia duty for conscientious objectors. Madison proposed: " . . . no person religiously scrupulous of bearing arms shall be compelled to render military service in person." This clause was approved by the House, but later rejected by a Senate conference committee.[33]

Although the Founding Fathers respected the rights of COs, they were concerned over who had the responsibility and power to exempt objectors from service. The Constitution did not grant Congress the explicit power to draft citizens into federal service. The Madison amendment gave to the federal government the power to insure that the rights of conscientious objectors were upheld by individual states.[34] States' rights advocates opposed the Madison amendment. They argued that states should maintain complete control over the composition of their own militias and that the federal government might abuse the CO exemption provision and use these powers to undermine state militias. Representative Eldridge Gerry opposed the amendment, stating: "They [the U.S. Congress] can declare who are those religiously scrupulous, and prevent them from bearing arms. . . . Whenever governments mean to invade the rights and liberties of the people, they always attempt to destroy the militia."[35]

At this time there was no standing U.S. Army as we know it today. The American National Army consisted of state militias which the President had the power to federalize and place under his control. The legal debate over whether Congress had the power to conscript was not resolved until 1918, when the Supreme Court upheld the constitutionality of the national draft.[36]

CONCLUSION

From the early days of colonial America, there were settlers who rejected violence in resolving disputes and refused to cooperate with the local militia system. These settlers were often instrumental in establishing freedom of conscience and civil rights in the New World. They also insured that new state governments, and ultimately the federal government, protected the rights of conscientious objectors.

But these early Quakers and pacifists were not war resisters in the modern understanding of that concept. Although they boldly refused to train or serve in the military despite laws and public pressure, they did not collectively protest the waging of war itself. Nor did they mobilize mass political resistance to the draft. When offered a legal exemption, they politely accepted. Their intent was not to stop war through collective action or public civil disobedience. Rather, their pacifism was an example and a personal religious statement for peace.

NOTES

1. Peter Brock, *Pacifism in the United States—From the Colonial Era to the First World War*, 21-80.
2. Adin Ballou, *Christian Non-Resistance in All Its Important Bearings*, 155-56. See also Brock, *Pacifism in the United States*, 35-36 (Indians not harming Quakers) and 165-66 (Indians murdering unarmed Mennonites); Beth Boyle, *Words of Conscience: Religious Statements on Conscientious Objection*, 16 (colonial nonresistance of members of the Church of the Brethren).
3. Brock, *Pacifism in the United States*, 55.
4. William L. Saunders, ed., *The Colonial Records of North Carolina, 1662–1776*, 1, 810-14. See also Margaret E. Hirst, *The Quakers in Peace and War*, 350-51.
5. See the "Charter of West New Jersey," reprinted in Richard Perry and John Cooper, eds., *Sources of Our Liberty: Documentary Origins of Individual Liberty in the United States Constitution and the Bill of Rights* (hereinafter ABA Documents).
6. Edwin P. Tanner, *The Province of West New Jersey, 1614–1738*, 563-75.
7. Brock, *Pacifism in the United States*, 61-62.
8. Gov. Dinwiddle to George Washington, letter of July 1, 1756, reprinted in John C. Fitzpatrick, ed., *The Writings of George Washington*, 1, 394n. 76.
9. Ibid., Washington to Dinwiddle, letter of August 4, 1756, 420.
10. Brock, *Pacifism in the United States*, 62.
11. ABA Documents, 170.
12. Hirst, *Quakers in Peace and War*, 330-40.
13. John Russell Bartlett, ed., *Records of the Colony of Rhode Is-*

land and Providence Plantations in New England, Statute of August 13, 1673.

14. Ibid.

15. Hirst, *Quakers in Peace and War*, 330-40.

16. Quakers were persecuted for scores of religious practices, including refusal to perform military service. See, for example, Elfrida Vipont, *The Story of Quakerism*, 40-41.

17. William Penn advocated many of the rights that were eventually granted criminal suspects under the U.S. Constitution. The famous Penn-Meade trial of 1670, in which a British or colonial jury refused to convict Penn and William Meade of the "crime" of preaching Quakerism in public and causing a riot, is considered a landmark case in establishing both religious liberty and the powers of juries in criminal trials. See, for example, *The Trial of William Penn and William Meade at the Old Bailey*, 6 State Trials 951, 22 Charles II (1670), and *The Case of the Imprisonment of Edward Bushell for Alleged Misconduct as a Juryman*, 6 State Trials 999, 22 Charles II (1670).

18. See Edward Channing, *A History of the United States*, in *A Century of Colonial History, 1660–1760*, 2, 322, cited in ABA Documents.

19. William Comfort, *William Penn and Our Liberties*.

20. William Penn, *The Rise and Progress of the Quakers*.

21. Isaac Sharpless, *A Quaker Experiment in Government*, 193, citing *Colonial Records of Pennsylvania*, 2, 470.

22. Ibid., 205; *Colonial Records of Pennsylvania*, 4, 366.

23. Ibid., 216.

24. Ibid., 217; *Colonial Records of Pennsylvania*, "Vote of the Assembly," 4, 501.

25. R. R. Russell, "Development of Conscientious Objection Recognition in the United States." 20 *George Washington Law Review* 409 (1951–1952).

26. Ibid.; see also the listings and commentary in *Macintosh v. U.S.*, 42 F.2d 845, 847 (1930); *Hamilton v. Regents*, 293 U.S. 245, 267 (Justice Cardozo concurrence, 1934).

27. 2 J. Cont. Cong. 189 (July 18, 1775). The statute read:

As there are some people, who, from religious principles, cannot bear arms in any case, this Congress intends no violence to their consciences, but earnestly recommends it to them to contribute liberally in time of universal calamity, to the relief of their distressed brethren in the several colonies, and do all other services to their religious principles.

28. Letter of January 19, 1777, in Fitzpatrick, *Writings of George Washington*, 3, 35; see also Washington to Council of Safety, letter of January 29, 1777, ibid., 79.

29. Brock, *Pacifism in the United States*, 238-39.

30. Ibid., 240.

31. Ibid., 183-284.

32. The states were North Carolina, Virginia, Rhode Island, and Pennsylvania. See *Elliots Debates*, 1, 334-35; 2, 531; 3, 657-59; 4, 243-44.

33. 1 *Annals of Congress* 434 (1789).

34. Bernard Schwartz, *The Great Rights of Mankind*, 160, 230; see also, for example, Leon Friedman, "Conscription and the Constitution: The Original Understanding," 67 *Mich. L.R.* 1493 (1969), and Michael Malbin, "Conscription, the Constitution and the Framers, An Historical Analysis," 40 *Fordham L.R.* 805 (1972).

35. Bernard Schwartz, *The Bill of Rights: A Documentary History*, 2, 1107.

36. The failure of the U.S. Constitution to explicitly include a provision allowing conscription led to serious challenges to the constitutionality of a federal draft. A number of important early authorities concluded that a national draft was unconstitutional. For example, the unpublished draft opinion of Roger Taney, the Chief Justice of the U.S. Supreme Court during the Civil War, concluded that the 1863 draft law was unconstitutional. (This opinion remained unpublished, for a constitutional challenge to the 1863 law never was argued before the Civil War court.) The Pennsylvania Supreme Court did address the issue of the constitutionality of a federal draft. In its first decision, the court found the law unconstitutional. But within a month of that decision, the composition of the court changed, and the Pennsylvania Supreme Court reversed itself. The U.S. Supreme Court did not uphold a federal draft until World War I. See Chief Justice Roger B. Taney, "Thoughts on the Conscription Law of the United States— Rough Draft Requiring Revision," *Tylers Quarterly Historical and Genealogical Magazine*, 18 (October 1936): 74-87; *Kneedle v. Lane*, 45 Pa. 238 (1863); Forrest Black, "The Selective Draft Cases, A Judicial Milepost on the Road to Absolutism," 11 *Boston University L.R.* 37 (September 19, 1931); James G. Randall, *Constitutional Problems Under Lincoln*; Friedman, "Conscription and the Constitution"; *Holmes v. U.S.*, 391 U.S. 936 (J. Douglas dissent); *Arver v. U.S.*, 245 U.S. 266 (1918); Philip Kurland, ed., *Landmark Briefs and Arguments of the Supreme Court of the United States: Constitutional Law*, 18, 575-827.

2

Draft Resistance and Abolitionism

During the late 1820s and early 1830s, America was shaken by a profound moral crusade—abolitionism. A new spirit of reform and social change erupted which revolutionized all future anti-draft movements. The anti-slavery movement planted the seed for a new peace movement that was more political, more radical, and more effective than any previous opposition to war.

Formerly, anti-draft activities were philosophically rooted in a sense of obedience to God, not disobedience to the laws of war. Whereas conscientious objection before the emergence of abolitionism was considered religious and personal, the absolutist crusade for peace was political and called for collective action. Abolitionists targeted the evil of war for active and aggressive political opposition. They sought to expand pacifism far beyond the passive noncompliance to war that the early settlers practiced.

"No compromise with evil" was the rallying call of abolitionism. Its initial target was slavery. Reform movements that attempted to humanize slavery by banning whippings or purchasing slaves for colonization in Africa were condemned. Led by William Lloyd Garrison, the new anti-slavery movement demanded nothing less than the immediate and unconditional abolition of slavery and full equality between the races.[1] In the beginning, the crusade was so unpopular it was banned in the South. In the North, abolitionists often met with ridicule, condemnation, and mob violence. At least one Northern abolitionist was murdered by an angry pro-slavery mob, and Garrison was nearly lynched in Boston.[2]

As an unpopular minority, the abolitionists developed protest tactics to stir up public opinion. They rallied to the Quaker notion of personal witness and noncooperation. Soon they took the next philosophical step to the belief that the immorality of slavery required every person to interfere with its daily operation and to work for its nonviolent overthrow. Newspapers were published, speeches and rallies held, runaway slaves assisted, and slave laws violated. Nonviolent direct action and civil disobedience replaced purely personal noncooperation.[3]

Many pacifist abolitionists viewed war as they did slavery. They considered it an uncompromisable evil. To oppose it, they borrowed tactics from the anti-slavery struggle and went further. Not only did they adopt the Quaker position of personal noncooperation with any war effort or organized militia system, but also they sought to openly oppose and frustrate government's ability to engage in war. One goal was to persuade the majority that war, like slavery, was a "sin" and that every person had a positive duty to prevent or stop it. In a remarkable document written by Garrison and adopted in 1838 as the Declaration of Sentiments of the New England Non-Resistance Society, the basic tenets of a new anti-war program were outlined. Garrison wrote:

We register our testimony, not only against all wars, whether offensive or defensive, but all preparations for war; against every naval ship, every arsenal, every fortification; against the militia system and a standing army; against all military chieftains and soldiers; against all monuments commemorative of victory over a foreign foe, all trophies won in battle, all celebrations in honor of military or naval exploits; against all appropriations for the defense of a nation by force and arms on the part of any legislative body; against every edict of government requiring of its subjects military service.[4]

The Declaration did not end with condemnation. It also called for mass civil disobedience to military laws and for political agitation against war appropriations. According to Garrison, people had a moral obligation to violate laws that supported the military. He outlined the basic tenets of modern civil disobedience: obey just laws and violate unjust laws; when the law is violated, accept punishment but do not compromise. The Declaration urged people to "obey all the requirements of government, except such as we deem contrary to the commands of the Gospel; and in no way resist the operation of laws except by meekly submitting to the penalty of disobedience."[5]

Garrison sought a mass civil disobedience campaign against warfare. He wrote:

While we shall adhere to the doctrines of non-resistance and passive submission to enemies, we propose, in a moral and spiritual sense, to speak and act boldly in the cause of God; to assail iniquity in high places and in low places; to apply our principles to all existing civil, political, legal, and ecclesiastical institutions.[6]

The abolitionist spirit revolutionized the earlier pacifist anti-draft position. Previously, conscientious objectors had requested some form of legal exemption from the draft. Only when these exemptions were denied or unavailable was the objector jailed. Garrison urged people to violate military laws. A Garrisonian resister would not seek legal methods to obtain exemption. Instead, he would break the "unjust" law and suffer the consequences. In Garrison's view, war was immoral, and all people shared a common responsibility to put an end to its beastly practices. No longer was pacifism perceived as part of a religious doctrine peculiar to Quakers, Mennonites, and other peaceful religions. Instead, pacifism was viewed as a moral imperative, and the campaign against the military was to be conducted by all people, regardless of religion or station in life. People had a positive duty to interfere with the military machine.

Just as the abolitionists were in the process of waging a nonviolent war against slavery—which included violating the fugitive slave acts of 1793[7] and 1850[8]—Garrison and the New England Non-Resistance Society envisioned a similar campaign against war. The pacifists/abolitionists took the spirit and program of the anti-slavery movement and transplanted it into the institution of war. Many abolitionists formulated complex schemes on how nonviolence could replace warfare. They felt nonviolence could be used to defeat domestic oppression and foreign armies alike. For example, Elihu Burritt, in his pamphlet *Passive Resistance*, argued that nonviolence could "crush any violent opposition."[9] Burritt pointed to a number of obscure historical incidents in which oppressed or invaded people had defended themselves with nonviolent direct action ("passive resistance").

One such incident occurred in the Sandwich Islands in the Pacific Ocean. The French had attempted to levy a tax, but the Islanders refused to pay. In anticipation of a French invasion, the island's leader ordered the people to "oppose no resistance" and refuse to fight against the invading army. When the French attacked, the people neither cooperated with nor fought against the occupying army. They simply went about their daily business while the army took "control" of the island. After a few frustrating days, the French left the island without collecting their tax. Burritt summed up this experience:

The simple, quiet force of *endurance* which the government opposed to the French wet their powder and turned their bayonets to straw. Against this unexpected force the marines were powerless. They had no arms to contend with such an enemy. All their weapons, and discipline, and bravery, were fitted only to overcome brute force.[10]

Garrison, Burritt, and other members of the Non-Resistance Society were pioneers in the development of the nonviolent, direct action strategy for social change.[11] Their methods and tactics inspired philosophers like Henry David Thoreau and Leo Tolstoy,[12] and were adopted later not only by the anti-draft movement but also by other great nonviolent movements, including Gandhi's movement for Indian independence and Martin Luther King, Jr.'s civil rights crusade.

Abolitionists were the first to formulate the philosophy of the modern anti-draft movement, but they failed to actively implement it in either the Mexican War (1846–1848) or the Civil War (1861–1865). Anti-slavery forces vigorously condemned the war against Mexico. They charged Southern states with provoking the war to conquer more slave territories. Abolitionists publicly advocated complete noncooperation with the military. Petitions were circulated calling on all signers to refuse any "aid, support, or countenance" for the war effort.[13] One such petition, signed by the anti-slavery leaders Wendell Phillips, Parker Phillsbury, Garrison, and others, called for civil disobedience and direct resistance to the war. It directed readers "at all hazards, and at every sacrifice to refuse enlistment, contribution, aid and countenance to the war."[14]

Although they called for nonviolent direct action, the abolitionists failed to mobilize public civil disobedience against it. (In the absence of a national draft law during the Mexican War, the concrete art of draft resistance was unavailable to them.) Historian John Schroeder, in his study of anti-war activities during the war with Mexico, summed up the failure of the abolitionists to organize mass nonviolent action. He wrote: "Although [the abolitionists] urged resistance to the government by withholding of all support, they made no active attempt to obstruct government policy. Nor did they make the symbolic step of refusing to pay their state tax, as Thoreau had done in 1846."[15] The abolitionists were primarily interested in the abolition of slavery. They never implemented their anti-war theories.

After the passage of the Fugitive Slave Act of 1850, bloody riots against its implementation and against the "kidnapping" of escaped slaves broke out in many Northern towns.[16] The "bleeding Kansas" controversy and John Brown's raid on Harper's Ferry, Virginia, also contributed to the erosion of the nonviolent ethic as it was associated with the abolitionist movement.[17] When the Civil War broke out in 1861, many former radical anti-war abolitionists laid aside their nonviolent convictions.[18]

Garrison never came out directly in support of the war. His newspaper continued to advocate peaceful methods of social change. But he did speak out strongly in favor of the war's anti-slavery goals. Garrison wrote, "Although non-resistance holds human life in all cases inviolable, yet it is perfectly consistent for those professing it to petition, advise, and strenuously urge a pro-war government to abolish slavery solely by the war power."[19]

During the nineteenth century, the philosophy of direct action against war did not merge with the Quaker/religious tactic of absolute noncooperation with war and the draft. Quakers and other religious minorities continued individually to
refuse conscription during the Civil War, but this resistance
never fused with a political ideology dedicated to frustrating
a government's ability to conduct a war. When no massive,
nonviolent, public disobedience to draft laws emerged, war resistance resumed its personal and religious character.

The major peace churches of the Mennonites and Quakers
steadfastly maintained their pacifist traditions. When the North
instituted a draft in 1863, religious objectors refused conscription and were jailed. Although President Lincoln personally
granted pardons to a number of Quakers who were inducted
or jailed, Northern resisters suffered abuse. The draft law was
amended on February 24, 1864, to include a conscientious objector exemption based on religious beliefs. After the exemption was passed, religious exemptions were granted liberally
because most of the objectors were sympathetic to the liberation of the slaves and readily accepted noncombat assignments in programs designed to aid the newly freed slaves.[20]

The South also passed a conscientious objector exemption to
its draft law. Although most religious objectors were exempted from service, a number of Southern objectors suffered
abuse. Mistreatment and ill-care led to the death of at least
one objector in a Southern military jail. Other incidents of abuse
included "piercing repeatedly [an objector] with a bayonet,
hanging up by the thumbs, beating and kicking, gagging with
an open bayonet, deprivation of sleep, long periods on a bread
and water diet, incarceration in filth," and the threatening of
prisoners with death by firing squad. Most of these tortures
were blamed on the "excessive zeal" of enlisted men or junior
officers.[21]

One fascinating account of draft resistance among the North
Carolina Society of Friends was reported in an 1863 letter
printed in the *Liberator*.[22] Twelve Friends refused a conscription order and were "unmercifully" tortured:

Every conceivable insult and outrage was heaped upon them; they
were tied up, starved, and whipped. Still they remained firm to their

conscientious convictions, and refused to fight. Finally, the muskets were absolutely strapped to their bodies.

One of these Friends was singled out as especially obnoxious, and was whipped unmercifully. The officer in charge was lawless and brutal, and on one occasion ordered him to be shot, as an example to others. He called out a file of men to shoot him. While his executioners were drawn up before him, standing within twelve feet of their victim, the latter, raising his eyes to heaven, and elevating his hands, cried out in a loud voice: "Father, forgive them, they know not what they do." Instantly came the order to fire. But, instead of obeying it, the men dropped their muskets and refused, declaring that they could not kill such a man.

The twelve objectors were forcibly marched with the rebel army into the battle of Gettysburg. During that battle, "they remained entirely passive" and never fired a shot. None of the Friends was injured, and all eventually were taken prisoner. Once under Northern jurisdiction, they obtained official discharges and were freed.

The famous anti-draft riots that broke out in the North were not organized or led by peace activists. Rioters were not influenced by pacifist principles. Rather, these riots were violent rebellions against the very goals of the Civil War and were led mainly by racist or pro-Southern whites. For example, the largest of the draft riots, the New York City uprising in the summer of 1863, turned into a pogrom against black residents of the city. Black people's homes and businesses were destroyed. Scores of blacks were murdered or brutally beaten on the streets. Eyewitness reports indicated that any black caught by the rioting mob was killed, regardless of age or sex. One contemporary account of the New York riot stated:

If [a Negro was] overtaken, he was pounded to death at once; if he escaped into a negro house for safety, it was set on fire, and the inmates made to share a common fate. . . . A negro lodging-house . . . was soon in ruins. Old men, seventy years of age, and young children, too young to comprehend what it all meant, were cruelly beaten and killed. . . . At one time there lay at the corner of Twenty-seventh Street and Seventh Avenue the dead body of a negro, stripped nearly naked, and around it a collection of Irishmen, absolutely dancing or shouting like wild Indians. . . . Deeds were done and sights witnessed that one would not have dreamed of.[23]

After the riots, the homes of at least 5,000 blacks were destroyed. Over 12,000 black riot victims were aided by a New York Merchants' charity drive.[24]

These riots are distinguished from every other anti-draft movement in American history: they were violent, and they were not based on anti-war or peace principles. Many protesters were hostile to the idea of fighting against whites to free blacks. Others resented the ability of the rich to hire "substitutes" while the poor had to fight.[25] Still others simply were tired of the Civil War. Garrison's *Liberator* critically characterized the anti-draft riots, noting that "The draft [was] only the pretext, not the real cause for this treasonable outbreak, which owes its origin and stimulus to that brutal hatred of the colored race."[26]

CONCLUSION

Although Garrison's philosophy and tactic of "nonresistance to evil" was not put into practice during the Civil War, it had a profound impact on all future generations of draft resisters. Fifty years after Garrison wrote the Declaration of Sentiments, Leo Tolstoy declared:

Garrison was the first to proclaim the principle [i.e. nonviolent direct action against evil] as a rule for the organization of the life of men. In this is his great merit. If at the time he did not attain the pacifist liberation of the slaves in America, he indicated the way of liberating men in general from the power of brute force.[27]

In World War I, the abolitionist dream of an anti-war campaign based on noncooperation and direct action was realized. A small but dynamic group of youthful draft resisters would merge the Quaker tactic of noncooperation with the Garrisonian tactic of nonviolent resistance. This merger laid the foundation for the birth of the modern anti-draft movement.

NOTES

1. Samuel May, *Some Recollections of Our Anti-Slavery Conflict*, 15-38 and 85-97.

2. Ibid., in the following chapters: "Reign of Terror," 150-57; "Riot in Utica," 162-70; "Gag Law," 185-202; "Murder of Lovejoy," 221-30; see also Joel T. Headley, *Pen and Pencil Sketches of the Great Riots*, 79-96 (hereinafter *Great Riots*).

3. See, for example, Peter Brock, *Pacifism in the United States— from the Colonial Era to the First World War*, especially his chapter on nonviolent resistance during the abolitionist period. See also Staughton Lynd, ed., *Nonviolence in America: A Documentary History*, 25-108.

4. William Lloyd Garrison, *Declaration of Sentiments*, reprinted in Lynd, *Nonviolence in America*, 25-31.

5. Ibid., 29.

6. Ibid., 29.

7. Act of February 12, 1793 ch. 7, 1 Stat. 302 (1793).

8. Act of 1850 ch. 60, 9 Stat. 462 (1850) (repealed, 1864). For information on resistance to the fugitive slave laws/Act, see also May, *Some Recollections*, 373-84 and Samuel May, *The Fugitive Slave Law and Its Victims*.

9. Elihu Burritt, *Passive Resistance*, reprinted in Lynd, *Nonviolence in America*, 93.

10. Ibid., 95.

11. See, for example, Abin Ballou, *Evils of the Revolutionary War*.

12. Leo Tolstoy, "Letter to V. Tchentkoff," reprinted as "On the Negro Question" in *Tolstoy's Writings on Civil Disobedience and Non-Violence*, 337-38.

13. See generally John H. Schroeder, *Mr. Polk's War: American Opposition and Dissent: 1846–1848*.

14. *The Liberator*, May 22, 1846.

15. Schroeder, *Mr. Polk's War*, 105-6.

16. May, *Recollections*, 373-84.

17. Brock, *Pacifism in the United States*, 667-85.

18. Ibid., 689-712.

19. Ibid., 698-99.

20. James G. Randall, *Constitutional Problems Under Lincoln*, 262; see also *U.S. Statutes at Large*, 38th Congress, Sess. I, ch. 13 (1864), 9.

21. Brock, *Pacifism in the United States*, 773-74; Arthur G. Sharp, "Men of Peace," *Civil War Times* (June 1982).

22. Letter of Alfred Love, *The Liberator*, August 21, 1863.

23. Headley, *Great Riots*, 207-8.

24. *Report of the Committee of Merchants for the Relief of Colored People Suffering from the Late Riots in the City of New York*, 7-10.

25. Ibid., 136-277, especially the "Closing Scenes" chapter which documents specific violence against black citizens, 273-78.

26. *The Liberator*, July 17, 1863; *The Liberator* reported on the massive violence against blacks, quoting from the *Boston Transcript*.

27. Tolstoy, *Tolstoy's Writings on Civil Disobedience*, 383.

3

World War I and the Birth of the Modern Movement

In human terms, World War I was tragic—8.5 million dead soldiers and 12.6 million dead civilians.[1] In terms of world peace, the war was a fiasco. Sold to the people of the West as the "war to end all wars" and the "war to make the world safe for democracy," it accomplished neither objective.[2] In fact, the treaties signed at the end of World War I strengthened colonialism, imperialism, and the spheres of influence that caused the war.[3] The inequities of the Treaty of Versailles laid the groundwork for the rise of Hitler's Germany. The League of Nations and other international peacekeeping mechanisms established after the war proved impotent. Instead of a world "safe for democracy," fascism, racism, and totalitarianism took hold of most of the earth. Wars were not ended. Instead, the path to the most bloody conflict in human history was carefully laid.[4]

The United States entered World War I on April 6, 1917. Within two months, the first national draft since the Civil War was signed into law.[5] Unlike modern draft laws, induction was not regulated by local draft boards. Instead, young men were inducted directly into the army and subjected to military rules. Conscientious objectors could either request combat exemptions from military officials or resist and face courts-martial.[6]

Only a handful of inductees either resisted military rule or applied for CO status. Of the 2.8 million men inducted into the armed services, a mere 3,500 obtained legal CO exemptions from active combat duty. A much smaller number became absolutists and resisted all military authority.[7]

The armed services convicted 450 "absolutist" war resisters at courts-martial. They were charged with crimes such as refusing to carry a rifle, refusal to train or follow orders, and failure to wear military uniforms. Although the absolutists could not cooperate with the military because of deeply held religious and political beliefs, their offenses were considered equivalent to treason and desertion. Many of the resisters, when convicted, were sentenced to death or life imprisonment for the crime of refusing to join the army.

Court-martialed resisters came from a wide variety of religious and political persuasions, including Mennonites, Dunkards, Quakers, Huttrians, socialists, anarchists, Molokans, "humanitarians," and members of the Industrial Workers of the World labor union. But regardless of their diverse backgrounds, they were united by a deep abhorrence of war and an absolutist refusal to cooperate with the military establishment.[8]

For the first time in American history, the Quaker tactic of draft noncooperation was merged with the abolitionist tactic of direct action. Instead of seeking to *avoid* the draft or military combat, resisters courted prosecution. Many refused to apply for or accept noncombatant service. They took a position similar to workers who go on strike: they refused to participate within a system in order to frustrate that system's ability to function.

Many absolutists made it perfectly clear to the military that they had no intention of applying for conscientious objector status. Jacob Wortsman, a socialist objector, bluntly informed the officers at his court-martial:

I cannot accept military service in any capacity or perform work of any sort under compulsion. . . . We cannot propagate our ideas by killing those who do not agree with us and by cowing a nation into submission. . . . I remain firm by my conviction and will suffer any length of incarceration and any amount of persecution in preference to submitting to a violation of my principles.[9]

Wortsman received a twenty-year sentence.

Roger Nash Baldwin, one of America's leading civil libertarians and a founder of the American Civil Liberties Union (ACLU), expressed similar sentiments at his 1918 draft trial. He articulated the new resistance philosophy by advocating civil disobedience:

I am not seeking to evade the draft; [I] scorn evasion, compromise, and gambling with moral issues. . . . I am opposed to any service under conscription . . . I can make no moral distinction between the various services which assist in prosecuting the war—whether rendered in the trenches, in the purchase of bonds or in the raising of farm products. . . . [This is] just one protest in a great revolt surging up from the people.[10]

Baldwin served ten months in jail for refusing to register for the draft. Upon release, he led political amnesty and defense campaigns on behalf of imprisoned COs.

The Military Intelligence Division (MID) considered Baldwin an "enemy of the government"[11] and kept him under constant surveillance during World War I. One plan considered by the MID was an indictment of Baldwin under the Espionage and Sedition Act. But the intelligence branch rejected this proposal. In a memo, a MID officer wrote, "It is also clear from my knowledge of Baldwin and his methods of operation that he would welcome an opportunity to pose as a martyr and very likely would be somewhat pleased at the prospect of spending a year or two at Atlanta penitentiary."[12] Baldwin was never indicted under the Espionage Act and remained a vocal advocate for the imprisoned objectors.

In an interview conducted shortly before his death in 1981, Baldwin described the importance of the absolutist stand against war and conscription. Absolute noncooperation, he said, has a "spiritual power"—a power that could be converted into an important political force:[13]

[Prisoners of conscience] have a certain social significance beyond the evidence, beyond these few men . . . they are just surface indications of something great and strong. It is the affirmation of a prin-

ciple. It is the affirmation of principles that have proved to be socially useful. It gives your principles a reality. . . . If you say, "Here
I stand, I can do no other," it is an important social force, and great
human history has been written by people who would not be moved.

The World War I objectors were the first American draft resisters to combine civil disobedience to war with a personal
absolutist refusal to enlist. Their faith in this tactic was not
grounded in pragmatic politics or an "objective" analysis of the
existing political environment. Instead, it was based on faith
in the "social force" behind civil disobedience—a belief in the
power of individuals and the ability of individual action to inspire others to follow boldly.

LEGAL REPRESSION

During World War I, both the courts and the military feared
that an effective noncooperation movement might hinder the
war effort. A number of judges and military officers used this
fear (or excuse) to justify long sentences for, and mistreatment of, the absolutist objectors. For example, District Court
Judge Julius Mayer, when he sentenced Roger Baldwin for draft
resistance, condemned the absolutist stand:

I cannot emphasize too strongly that in my view, not only could this
war not have been successfully and in a self-respecting way carried
on by the United States Government if such an attitude as yours
[Baldwin's] had prevailed, but I think such an attitude would have
led inevitably to disorder and finally to the destruction of the government.[14]

The military authorities directly ordered the court-martiall-
ing of anti-war activists. In a military order dated April 27,
1918, the Secretary of War commanded local military officials
to court-martial any conscientious objector who was "active in
propaganda" or "sullen and defiant."[15] After this order, almost all absolutists were court-martialed and sentenced to extremely long terms in military prisons. According to Department of War statistics, a total of 450 COs were found guilty
at these military hearings. Seventeen COs were sentenced to

death (all these death sentences were later commuted), 142 were sentenced to life in prison, and 73 were given twenty-year terms. Only fifteen objectors were sentenced to three years' imprisonment or less.[16]

The long sentences were coupled with incarceration in some of the worst prisons in the United States, such as Fort Leavenworth and Alcatraz Island.

TORTURE AND MISTREATMENT

The treatment of the imprisoned World War I resisters was barbaric. At least seventeen objectors died in jail as a direct consequence of torture or poor prison conditions.[17] Others were driven insane. Common punishment for COs (and other military prisoners) consisted of two consecutive weeks in solitary confinement on a bread and water diet in a completely dark cell, chained or handcuffed to the wall for nine hours each day.[18] Objectors were imprisoned in unsanitary guardhouses, often without blankets in unheated cells during the winter months. "Men were forcibly clad in uniform, beaten, pricked or stabbed with bayonets, jerked about with ropes around their necks, threatened with summary execution. . . . In at least two cases, men were immersed in the filth of latrines."[19]

A number of military officers justified these conditions as appropriate treatment for dangerous enemies of the state. In a revealing letter the commanding officer at Camp Fuson, Kansas, a camp notorious for its mistreatment of COs, urged their harsh treatment:

Not only are they refusing to play the part of loyal citizens, but they are also, by work and example, spreading discontent among other men. Their conduct is reprehensible in the highest degree, and if men of this character, in fact, enemies of the government, are not dealt with vigorously, their evil influence will be far reaching."[20]

Another example of the military's attitude toward COs came from the Military Intelligence Office in Dallas, Texas. A memorandum for that office referred to COs an "animals" and stated that "no measures taken can be too severe for this type of man."[21]

The military had only contempt for organizations that supported the COs. For example, Captain J. Hatheway of the Military Morals Section strongly condemned the American Union Against Militarism and the National Civil Liberties Bureau. Hatheway urged the complete repression of these organizations, writing in a memo: "An effort must be made to stop their propaganda at its very source. Their influence is pernicious and the organizations should be put out of business. Until then we shall have to deal with a very troublesome breed of objectors."[22]

In the face of torture, mistreatment, and social isolation, it is difficult to fully appreciate the courage and heroism of World War I objectors. They were imprisoned at a time when there was no strong active base within the population to support their position. They operated in a political vacuum in a period when patriotic feelings about such threats as "the Red Scare" reached hysterical proportions.[23]

Many objectors wrote diaries or letters describing their torture behind bars.[24] Four representative cases of abuse, based on notes the COs made at the time or newspaper accounts, are sketched below:

PHILIP GROSSER, a political objector, was sentenced to thirty years' imprisonment for being an absolutist CO. Grosser faced solitary confinement in every prison in which he served.[25] A letter smuggled out of the guardhouse at Fort Andrews describes how he was hanged nearly to death:

The hemp band was put around my neck and I was made to swing. . . . I was beaten black and blue, kicked and jumped upon. . . . I am ready to suffer the supreme penalty with a smile on my face. But damn if they will make me observe military rules by force. . . . My will power is stronger than the bayonet and my ideas will not be shot out of my head.[26]

At Alcatraz, he was placed in solitary confinement as punishment for his refusal to break rocks. He wrote:

The hardest things to endure in the dungeon were the complete darkness, the sitting and sleeping on the damp concrete floor, and the lack of sight and sound of any human being. The eighteen ounces of bread was quite sufficient for the first few days. . . . The rats were quite peaceful and friendly.

Solitary confinement could not break Grosser's spirit. He, along with a small group of absolutists, did not buckle under military discipline. In response, the prison administration constructed special "coffin cages" for the COs. Coffin cages were used only against conscientious objectors at Alcatraz and were reportedly discarded after the COs were released from prison. Grosser, who spent more than two months in the coffin cages, described their make-up:

[The] cages were 23 inches wide and 12 inches deep. Each cage was made of iron bars bolted to the door of the cells. The prisoner [stood] upright, with an adjustable board to his back to reduce the depth to about 9 inches so as to make a tight fit—a veritable iron straight jacket.[27]

For two months Grosser spent eight hours a day in the cages. The remaining sixteen hours of each day were spent in solitary confinement on a bread and water diet. Realizing that neither his "brain nor body" could endure these tortures, Grosser finally agreed to work and was released from these brutal conditions.

ROBERT GAGE was sentenced to twenty-five years' imprisonment at a military court-martial. Gage rejected the legitimacy of military authority over his life. He would not cooperate with his jailers. At Leavenworth, Gage refused to work. This refusal angered guards who threatened him with bayonets. Sticking to his principles, Gage folded his arms while an officer readied and loaded his rifle:

I first received a rather hard blow from the bayonet which struck me over the left kidney. Then the sentry and sergeant took me by force outside the stockade. . . . I still refused to go to work and the Major repeated his orders. I received two more wounds but yet refused.[28]

Gage was treated at the prison infirmary where he remained ill and unable to eat for a number of days.

JULIUS FIRESTONE was a socialist leader from New York who

was inducted into the army. As a CO he was imprisoned at Camp Hancock, Georgia. There, soldiers angered by his anti-war convictions tarred and feathered him. He sickened because of this incident and died of pneumonia on November 25, 1918.[29]

ERNEST GELLERT was a sensitive young man from New Jersey. Unable to withstand the isolation and torment of confinement, he committed suicide. At his court-martial hearing, Gellert was questioned concerning his pacifist ideals. An almost prophetic exchange occurred between Gellert and the military hearing officer:

Officer [O]: You state that you are perfectly willing to take any punishment subsequent to violation of orders?

Gellert [G]: I am willing to take whatever consequence my attitude may bring.

O: You have no fear of death?

G: I am as much afraid of death as anybody else. To me death would mean the end of my existence. Perhaps I should be more afraid of death than ordinary people, but nevertheless, if death should be the alternative, I would submit to death.

O: You hold life sacred, above everything else?

G: When you reduce things to its terms, that is what we come to.

O: And you place your personal opinions above life?

G: My personal opinions and my life are synonymous.

Following his court-martial conviction, Gellert was denied family visits and subjected to almost constant ridicule from the enlisted men. This ridicule was a source of tremendous mental anguish for Gellert. He committed suicide. On April 8, 1918, Gellert's body was found with a note by its side:

I fear I have not succeeded in convincing the authorities of the sincerity of my scruples against participation in the war. I feel that only by my death will I be able to save others from the mental tortures I have gone through. If I succeed, I give my life willingly.[30]

Not surprisingly, the U.S. military had a very different conception of the cause of Gellert's death. A memorandum prepared by the chief of the Executive Division of Military Intelligence for E. P. Keppel, Third Assistant Secretary of War, said the army had shown "patience, sympathy, and tolerance" toward Gellert, and was not to blame. He assigned responsibility for Gellert's death to the National Civil Liberties Bureau. According to the memorandum: "The organization which encouraged and supported Gellert in his attitude and which is most to be blamed in the whole unfortunate affair is the National Civil Liberties Bureau."[31] In the same memo, the Civil Liberties Bureau was also charged with "exploiting Gellert's death" in order to "encourage opposition to the . . . war."

Most abuse against objectors was either officially sanctioned or, when committed by zealous enlisted men, went unpunished. But there are a scattering of cases in which mistreatment of COs was officially reprimanded. In one instance, after protests from the Seventh Day Adventist Church, a number of enlisted men were disciplined for beating a nonabsolutist church member. According to the MID, the enlisted men had "made [the objector] wear a placard bearing the inscription 'I am yellow,' and severely beat [the objector]."[32] No mention was made as to the type of punishment imposed on the enlisted men.

PRISON REBELLION AND REFORM: THE FORT LEAVENWORTH GENERAL STRIKE

COs are not average prisoners. Few, if any, have previous criminal records. Many are well educated and articulate, possessing organizing skills and political connections. For the most part, they are radical idealists with strong humanitarian philosophies. World War I witnessed the first confrontation between COs and the prison system.

Resisters during World War I started a CO tradition of prison protest campaigns and strikes. Small nonviolent prison strikes and protest actions occurred at a scattering of prison camps during the war. But serious trouble unfolded when the vast majority of COs were collected from around the country and herded into the Fort Leavenworth "concentration camp" in November 1918. The armed services ordered the centralized

confinement of objectors, in part to better control and spy on
them. The MID thought that Fort Leavenworth would become
a gold mine for the intelligence service. An MID memo reads:

Fort Leavenworth is about to become the Concentration Camp for
Conscientious Objectors. . . . From the viewpoint of the Intelligence
Service, the coming of the Conscientious Objectors will afford a de-
cidedly fertile field for activities. These men will undoubtedly have a
wealth of information of value to the Intelligence Service, and their
presence will enable us to gain a more complete knowledge of Social-
istic and Anarchistic activities; Religious and Industrial Organizations, etc.[33]

The MID laid detailed plans for "camouflaging"military spies
as COs and planting them among the Leavenworth prison
population. The MID suggested that undercover operatives read
radical books by Trotsky and mail a letter to the National Civil
Liberties Bureau stating their fake reasons for objecting to
military service. Once an identity as an objector was established, the operative was directed to "cultivate a slouch" and
"overcome the snap and precision of military training in order
to melt into the ranks of COs."[34] The memo does not discuss
the final outcome of these spying escapades.

In November 1918, the Leavenworth COs staged their first
work strike. Twenty-four objectors refused to work in order to
protest the gross mistreatment of Molokan religious COs. The
Molokans, members of a small Russian pacifist religious sect,
could neither speak nor write English. Consequently, they were
almost totally isolated from outside support.[35] Remaining true
to the principles of their church, the Molokans refused all work
assignments at Fort Leavenworth. As a result, they were placed
in solitary confinement, manacled to their cell walls for nine
hours every day, placed on a diet of bread and water, and badly
beaten by guards.

The CO population at Leavenworth became concerned over
the plight of the Molokans. Evan Thomas, a religious objector
and the brother of the famous socialist leader Norman Thomas,
complained to Leavenworth Warden Colonel Sedgwick Rice and
insisted on the release of the Molokans from solitary confine-

ment. Colonel Rice rejected Thomas' plea. In a display of solidarity with the Molokans, Thomas refused to work. He was joined by twenty-three other objectors. All were sent into the "hole."

The striking COs secretly slipped information blasting the inhuman conditions in solitary to their nonstriking comrades within the prison population. Clark Getts, who along with Carl Haessler was reputed to be the mastermind of prison mail smuggling, leaked reports of the conditions to the National Civil Liberties Bureau. In one such report, dated November 14, 1918, Getts wrote:

The Hole in our jail [is a] black cold place in the subbasement. The men there are chained by their wrists to their cell doors for nine hours a day. They sleep on a cold cement floor between folded blankets and are given bread and water if they will eat at all. There is brutality enough, too. I saw one man dragged by his collar across the right corridor floor, screaming and choking. . . . Several [Molokans] have been hunger striking in the Hole. Two of them were beaten so beastly that even the authorities were shocked . . . other beatings and tortures are matters of general knowledge.[36]

Getts pleaded with outside supporters to pressure the government in Washington to stop the mistreatment. The objectors' supporters issued vehement protests before the government and Department of War. These efforts resulted in a Department of War memorandum dated December 6, 1918, which abolished forever the military policy of manacling defiant prisoners in solitary confinement to the walls of their cells.[37] Shortly thereafter, all of the Molokans and protesting objectors were released from solitary confinement. The War Department commuted Thomas' sentence and ordered his release from Leavenworth. After two months, the first prison strike at Leavenworth had been a complete success. Emboldened by this example, the entire inmate population gained a new respect for the war resisters. The stage was set for the Leavenworth general strike.

Interspersed among the general prison population of over 3,000 were approximately 300 COs. Abhorrent prison conditions confronted both COs and regular prisoners alike. The prison was overcrowded; working, eating, recreation facilities, and living conditions were archaic. Discipline was extreme.[38] Adding to this tension was the feeling among prisoners that they had been sentenced in excess of what their "crimes" deserved. Abysmal conditions and ridiculously long sentences (twenty years for refusing to peel potatoes) affected COs and non-COs alike.

The strike was precipitated by the death of two members of the Huttrian Brotherhood, a branch of the Mennonite Church. The Huttrians were transferred to Leavenworth after a long and debilitating stay in solitary confinement at Alcatraz. Although sick and physically broken from their Alcatraz punishments, the Huttrians continued to refuse all work. They were sent into the Leavenworth "hole." Within a period of days, two of the Huttrians died.[39] This incident outraged the prison population.

On Wednesday, January 29, 1919, one hundred and fifty members of the "first work gang" spontaneously walked off their jobs. Leaderless, they returned to their cells. The prison officials made no attempt to force these inmates back to work. That evening the entire prison population was humming with talk of rebellion and general strike. Everyone felt the frustration of confinement and yet did not know how to direct these energies:

No one had formulated that afternoon any statement of what was wanted. One prisoner wanted more tobacco; another wanted better food . . . a fifth wanted the privilege of writing more letters . . . absorption in small desires, and utter disagreement of one man to another, characterized the early stages of the strike.[40]

Colonel Rice, the warden, met informally with the inmates the next morning. He informed them that mass refusal to work was mutiny—a crime punishable by death. Rice threatened to call out 4,000 troops, warning that a strike would be futile and counterproductive. By the time Rice finished threatening the inmates, the obstacles confronting them appeared insurmountable.

That afternoon, 2,300 inmates were lined up for work. When

an officer called for the first work gang, a yell came back from
the prisoners: "There ain't no first gang!" All the inmates stood
silently, many with their arms folded defiantly. Colonel Rice
called for an inmate to state the strikers' demands. No one
moved. All feared being identified as the leader and being shot
as an organizer of the "mutiny." The tension was broken when
a young objector, W. Oral James, stepped forward and addressed the warden:

> I am in no sense a leader of these men. I can speak for myself,
> however, and I think I speak for many others in these silent ranks
> when I say that our object in thus seeming to oppose authority is that
> this is the only way in which we can make articulate our demand to
> know what is to become of us?
>   I am a conscientious objector. I realize that in thus separating my-
> self from this mass I make myself a marked man among your offi-
> cers. I am willing to do this, sir, if I can enlighten this protest.

James went on to state that the prisoners' sentences were too
long. He ended the speech with a plea to Colonel Rice to make
their protest heard in Washington.

Rice issued a final order for the inmates to report to work.
An estimated one hundred inmates broke rank and reported.
The remaining 2,200 were marched back into their cells. That
evening both the military authorities and the prisoners organized. Colonel Rice received permission to use the troops of the
49th Infantry Regiment to "maintain discipline." One thousand armed soliders were readied for combat and sent to the
prison gate.

A reporter from *Survey* magazine coincidentally was present in Leavenworth writing a story about prison conditions
when the strike broke out. According to his accounts, the inmates perfected their organization in the seventh wing of
Leavenworth and duplicated a similar internal organization
throughout the prison's remaining wings. Each wing elected
its own committee and one inmate to serve on a general inmate committee. Demands were formulated and sent via mes-
sengers to the various wings for negotiation, discussion, and
consolidation. The *Survey* reporter, Winthrop Lane, described
some of the action unfolding in the seventh wing:

Simmons [a CO] mounted a box. . . . He told [the strikers] that
the strike had been organized in other wings. . . . He told them that
theirs was the just cause of self-government now being fought for
throughout the civilized world. . . . He declared that no authority
could withstand the power of a united body of men. . . . "Violence
accomplishes nothing," [Simmons said]. "Solidarity accomplishes all
things. The watchword of the working men throughout the world today is solidarity. Say nothing, do nothing, but stand like this." The
speaker folded his arms. "A man who commits no overt act, but stands
like this, is immovable."

The *Survey* reporter recollected:

As he spoke, I thought of the thick walls that shut these men in, and
of the barred doors between them and their fellows. I wondered what
was the mysterious power by which the speaker and his listeners
thought they could control their own destinies.[41]

The following morning Colonel Rice met with the elected
general strike committee. Rice was presented with three demands: (1) amnesty for the strike leaders and release of all
inmates from solitary; (2) recognition of the permanent grievance committee; and (3) a recommendation by the colonel to
the War Department in Washington, D.C., that all the military prisoners be released immediately.

Rice shocked the inmates. First, he read from a telegram he
had already sent to Washington urging the reduction of excessive military sentences. He informed the committee that he
would personally go to Washington to deliver the strikers'
message. He agreed to the amnesty demand and to the recognition of an elected inmate grievance committee. Within four
hours the prisoners voted unanimously to return to work.

Following Rice's return from Washington, 60.6 percent of the
COs had their sentences reduced; another 33 percent were released immediately; and only 6.4 percent of the COs did not
receive a sentence reduction. As a result of these commuta-
tions, the last of the COs was released from miltary prison in
November 1920. None of the long sentences was carried out.

A General Prison Conference Committee was elected. It accomplished the following reforms:

- The internal prison judicial system was revamped. Sentences for infractions were reduced, and prisoners were granted the right to present evidence and to be represented by another inmate.
- A campaign to eliminate bed-bugs was initiated.
- Food was improved. The grains and cattle raised on the prison farm were allocated to the inmates as well as to the military officers who previously were their sole consumers.
- Letter writing privileges were expanded, and censorship was limited.

A nonviolent prison rebellion had succeeded. This "mutiny" was the pinnacle of the movement of World War I war resisters for nonviolent direct action. The strike reinforced the faith of many resisters in nonviolent action and was one of the few bright spots in their tortuous experiences during that war.[42]

But the progressive results of the strike were short-lived. Once the COs were transferred out of Leavenworth, the prison administration reneged on the reforms. By July 1919 all strike leaders had either been released or transferred. The vast majority of COs also had been removed from the institution. In addition, over 1,000 new military prisoners were added to the general population. Many of these new inmates, fresh from the front lines in France, were reportedly in an "ugly" mood. The military had promised these soldiers early release, but instead they found themselves crowded into Fort Leavenworth. The situation was tense.

On July 20, 1919, a minor incident (the transfer of a popular inmate from Leavenworth to Alcatraz) triggered a work strike. The administration's response was swift and repressive. Every prisoner, even those who did not support the strike, was locked up and placed on a bread and water diet. The elected inmate committee was disbanded, and the prison was transformed into a battle ground. According to an account:

In the riot-galleries, high over the door of each wing, sat sentries with shotguns across their knees. Through the windows they [the inmates] saw scores of sentries posted on the walls with machine guns pointed into the yard.

The prisoners were kept in lock-up on restricted diets. No one was allowed to bathe. Once a guard opened fire into the cell block, killing one inmate and wounding several others. After ten days the cells were individually searched; all nonprison-authorized materials were confiscated—including books, soap, and clothing. The inmates were informed that they had lost all their "good-time" and would be denied parole. Their spirits were completely broken. When the prisoners were finally taken from their cells, their heads were shaven. When ordered by the guards to work, none refused. The experiment in prison democracy had ended.[43]

CONCLUSION

Although COs completely failed to stop American involvement in World War I, the early resisters had a remarkable impact on all future draft resistance movements. Their example of courage, their tactics of complete noncooperation, their goals of frustrating induction, and their nonviolent ideals would inspire subsequent generations of resisters. For the first time in the history of U.S. conscription, the absolutist tactic used by the Quakers in colonial America was merged with the powerful nonviolent theory of the abolitionists. This synthesis gave birth to the modern anti-draft movement.

Norman Thomas, in his 1923 study of World War I COs, foresaw the historical significance of these absolutists:

No sympathetic historian of conscientious objection can speak of the past or of the future without emphasizing the significance of precisely that group of objectors which was most despised, derided, and persecuted. Their names will not be remembered, their deeds may be forgotten, yet if the day finally dawns when human society will be a fellowship of free men, not the least of the prophets and pioneers of that dawning will be the absolutists of 1918.[44]

Thomas correctly understood the pioneering role these COs played in the history of draft resistance and the peace movement.

NOTES

1. *Encyclopedia Britannica*, Vol. 28, 775.
2. Howard Zinn, *A People's History of the United States*, 352-55.
3. *Britannica*, Vol. 28, 791; William L. Shirer, *The Rise and Fall of the Third Reich*, 89-97.
4. Ibid.
5. Norman Thomas, *Is Conscience a Crime?*, 73-81; *International Socialist Review*, 1917.
6. For an explanation of these procedures, see *Estep v. U.S.*, 327 U.S.114, 132 N.1 (1946); Thomas, *Conscience*, 73-127. The U.S. government commited numerous gross violations of basic due process during its prosecution of World War I draft cases. For example, Ben Salmon, a Catholic conscientious objector, was convicted of refusing to complete an Army questionnaire in federal district court. He was sentenced to nine months imprisonment and was freed on bond pending appeal. Although he was never officially inducted into the army, he was arrested by local police and turned over to military authorities. Salmon was denied the opportunity to talk with either his family or his attorney and was locked up in a guard house. Despite the military's lack of jurisdiction over him, and the illegality of his confinement, Salmon was court-martialed and sentenced to twenty-five years hard labor for "desertion and propaganda." His writ of *habeas corpus* to the U.S. District Court in the District of Columbia was denied without a full written opinion. Salmon refused to cooperate with the Army authorities, and participated in work strikes and a four-month hunger strike. In retaliation, the military transferred Salmon to the St. Elizabeth's Hospital for the Insane where he was involuntarily confined on the ward for the "criminally insane." After serving over two years in military jails and St. Elizabeth's he was released by order of the Secretary of War on November 24, 1920. For the complete story of Salmon's imprisonment see Torin Finney, *Practical Catholic*, 18-42.
7. Secretary of War, *Statement Concerning the Treatment of Conscientious Objectors in the Army*, 25. Beyond those arrested for violation of draft laws, thousands of other anti-war socialists and radicals were arrested under the Espionage and Sedition Act; see, for example, Robert J. Goldstein, *Political Repression in Modern America: 1870 to the Present*, 103-31, and Zechariah Chaffe, Jr., *Freedom of Speech*.
8. *New York Times*, January 22, 1919; *New York World*, November 26, 1920; Francis Hennessy, letter dated October 7, 1918, ACLU

Collection at Princeton University Library (hereinafter ACLU); American Civil Liberties Union, *Conscientious Objectors: The Facts Today*, ACLU, 1920; American Civil Liberties Union, *Conscientious Objectors Who Died in Prison*, ACLU, February 6, 1920; *Chicago Tribune*, December 18, 1918; *New York Call*, November 26, 1918.

9. Jacob Wortsman, *Statement to Jury at Court Martial*, ACLU, 1917.

10. Roger Nash Baldwin, *The Individual and the State*, ACLU, 1918, 7-8.

11. Military Intelligence Division (MID), File No. 10902, July 18, 1918.

12. MID File No. 76-84, *Memo from Capt. Lester to Major Hunt*, August 24, 1918.

13. Interview conducted by the author, Summer 1981.

14. Baldwin, *The Individual and the State*, 14.

15. Secretary of War, *Statement*, 19.

16. Ibid., 51.

17. The objectors who died in jail were: Charles W. Bolly, Frank Burke, Reuben J. Eash, Julius Firestone, Daniel B. Flory, Henery E. Franz, Ernest Gelert, Joseph and Michael Hofer (brothers), Johannes M. Klassen, Van Skedine, Walter Sprunger, Daniel E. Teuscher, Mark R. Thomas, Ernest D. Wells, John Wolfe, and Daniel S. Yoder. Twelve of these COs were religious pacifists, three were socialists, and the remaining two were of unknown faith or political persuasion. These names were obtained from the following lists and articles: David Hofer, *Desecration of the Dead*, ACLU, undated; H. Austin Simons, "Fifth Objector Dies," *New York Call*, October 12, 1919; "COs Who Died in Prison," ACLU, February 6, 1920; *New York Call*, November 26, 1918; Walter Nelles, "Letter to Woodrow Wilson," ACLU, May 13, 1918.

18. Thomas, *Conscience*, 143-64.

19. Ibid., 144.

20. *New York Call*, January 11, 1919.

21. MID File No. 10902-1136.

22. Ibid., File No. 76-84.

23. Goldstein, *Political Repression*, 103-31; Chaffe, *Freedom of Speech*.

24. The ACLU collection at Princeton University has a remarkable selection of these materials on public file.

25. Philip Grosser, *Uncle Sam's Devil's Island*.

26. Ibid.; see also Grosser, letters dated February 24, 1918, February 28, 1918, and March 26, 1918, ACLU, 1918.

27. Grosser, letters dated February 24 and 28, 1918, ACLU, 1918.

28. Robert Gage, undated letter, ACLU, 1919.

29. *New York Call*, November 26, 1918.

30. Nelles, "Letter to Wilson."

31. MID, Churchill to Keppel, File No. 10902-38.

32. MID, IO-Camp Devens, File No. 10902-13.

33. Ibid.; MID, IO Camp Leavenworth to Central Department, File No. 10902-77.

34. Ibid., undated memo to Colonel Mastelle.

35. Thomas, *Conscience*, 188-203.

36. Clark Getts, letter dated November 14, 1918, ACLU.

37. Thomas, *Conscience*, 195-96.

38. Winthrop Lane, *Survey*, February 15, 1919. Lane was at a Leavenworth during the strike. The subsequent account in this book is based primarily on Lane's account.

39. Hofer, *Desecration*.

40. Lane, *Survey*.

41. Ibid.

42. H. Austin Simons, *The Second Strike at Ft. Leavenworth*, ACLU, 1919.

43. Ibid.

44. Thomas, *Conscience*, 292.

4

World War II and the Continuation of the Pacifist Tradition

World War II was the bloodiest conflict in human history, bringing devastation to three continents. Millions were slaughtered in concentration camps, while hundreds of thousands of noncombatants burned during massive bombing raids on civilian targets. The tragedy of Dresden was matched by the tragedy of Warsaw. Modern war psychology and technology resulted in the deaths of between 35 and 60 million people. World War II began with the madness of conquest, only to end with the madness of nuclear war. Conscientious objectors were outcasts in a world reduced to hell. The American war resister stood alone in a nation convinced of the necessity, the inevitability, and the glory of the war. The objectors had a message of nonviolence, despite the violence that wracked the nations. Regardless of the logic of war, they maintained the logic of peace.

At first glance, nonviolent resistance to fascism may appear completely utopian. The Nazis brutally crushed dissent with torture, starvation, deportation, and mass executions. But even in the face of unparalleled barbarism, nonviolent tactics were successfully employed. The most famous example occurred in Denmark, where almost the entire Jewish population was saved from the Holocaust because the Danish King and people engaged in noncooperation with the Nazis.[1] Hundreds of thousands of Jews were also saved through nonviolence in other German-occupied states, including Bulgaria,[2] Greece,[3] Italy,[4] France,[5] Belgium,[6] Norway, and the Netherlands.[7]

Unfortunately, the converse was also true. Where native populations cooperated with fascist rule, there was unprecedented human tragedy. In her exhaustive study of national responses to Jewish victimization during World War II, Helen Fein concluded that the "principal intervening factor" in explaining the success of Jewish extermination in various fascist-controlled nations was the extent of cooperation between the German invaders and the occupied peoples.[8] Native resistance, where it occurred, checked Jewish extermination.[9] What the outcome would have been had Hitler met with well-organized and popular nonviolent resistance in Germany and in other occupied states in Europe is impossible to say. But the successes of nonviolent action in specific cases are well documented.

THE AMERICAN ANTI-DRAFT MOVEMENT

World War II was a tremendous test for the American nonviolent resistance movement. When the Civil War began in 1861, the pacifists/abolitionists allowed their hatred of slavery to blur their vision of peace. They should not be faulted for this, for the abolitionists were primarily an anti-slavery movement. The twentieth-century resisters, on the other hand, were concerned primarily with the abolition of war and violence against people. For them, violence was oppression, and war was the grossest form of violence. Even in the face of Hitler's fascism, the World War II resisters did not compromise their pacifist convictions.

By any account, conscientious objectors during World War II were a tiny proportion of the American draft-age population. Of the 34,506,923 men who registered for the draft, the Selective Service System estimated that only 72,354 applied for CO status. That is, less than two-tenths of 1 percent of the eligible age group requested the pacifist exemption. A majority of these 72,000 COs were never imprisoned. Approximately 25,000 entered the army in noncombatant service, and another 11,950 were assigned to alternative service in civilian work camps. An estimated 20,000 potential COs did not receive official CO status. Some saw their claims denied by a local board and were forced to enter the armed services. Others won exemption because of their occupations or their dependents. Ultimately, 6,086 COs were imprisoned for violating the Selective Service Act.[10]

Only a minority of the imprisoned COs were in fact war resisters. Many were Jehovah's Witnesses, who did not claim to be absolutist objectors and were not imprisoned for taking a political anti-war stand. Most draft boards refused to give Witnesses ministerial exemptions, offering CO exemptions instead. When Witnesses registered for the draft, they remained firm in their religious tenets which held that all members were ministers. Most of the imprisoned Witnesses refused to accept any exemption but ministerial. Hence, Witnesses primarily went to prison not because of anti-war convictions, but because of religious misunderstanding, prejudice, and persecution.[11] If Jehovah's Witnesses are excluded from the category of "war resister," the total number of absolutist war resisters was aproximately 1,675.[12] (See Table 1.)

Not surprisingly, American wartime society mocked and

Table 1
Convictions for Violating the Selective Service Act from 1940 to 1946, by Faith or Religion

Faith or Religion*	Number of Convictions
Jehovah's Witnesses	4,441
Negro "Moslems," "Hebrews," etc.	167
Members of large religious groups	522
Members of small religious groups	310
Members of no religion	316
Political, philosophical, etc.	255
Not classified	105
Total	6,116

*Classifications are those of the Selective Service System/ Department of Justice.

Source: Selective Service System, *Conscientious Objectors Special Monograph No. 11*, 263; U.S. Bureau of the Census, *Historical Statistics of the United States*, 1143.

ridiculed war resisters. As a tiny minority, the resisters' ideals seemed alien to mainstream public opinion. For example,
one magazine article referred to the imprisoned absolutists as
"egomaniacs, psychopaths, eccentrics, and saboteurs," whose
political ideas were "highly ethereal and fanatical" with "little
contact with anything earthly and realistic."[13] War resisters
were also considered dangerous to national security. Both the
Federal Bureau of Investigation (FBI) and the Military Intelligence Division (MID) kept a careful watch on the anti-draft
movement.

    Government agencies compiled hundreds of detailed records
on resisters. Before resister Larry Gara turned eighteen, for
example, the MID had opened a file that gave his complete
personal history, including his "habits," "associates," "method
of operation," references to a letter Gara had mailed to a congressman, and a detailed physical description.[14] Among the
documents in the report was a transcript of a paper Gara had
submitted to the administration of his local high school. An
MID memo expressed considerable concern over Gara's interpretation of the pledge of allegiance. Gara had written:

When I do pledge allegiance to the flag, I am pledging allegiance to
the good things that America stands for, I am pledging allegiance to
those who believe in the power of love over the power of force, not to
those who are profiteering in the munitions industries. . . . I am
pledging allegiance not to the vain commercial patriotism of "God Bless
America," but rather to the lasting beauty of "America the Beauti-
ful." . . . I am pledging allegiance to the thousands of Negroes who
are deprived of their right to vote.

The MID urged continuous surveillance of Gara, warning that
the "subject" may "try to collect groups of people to march on
public offices protesting any bills or acts that are not within
his belief."

    Gara served three years in jail for refusing to register for
the draft. In 1949 he was convicted and imprisoned for counseling a young man not to register for the draft. Still an active
member of the peace movement, Gara today teaches History
and Peace Studies at Wilmington College in Ohio.[15]

THE IDEALS OF THE MOVEMENT

At the time of the war, young peace activists were inspired by the ability of idealists, like the abolitionists, to achieve meaningful social change despite their minority status. The new pacifists praised the radicals of the past. A pamphlet published in 1940 by sixteen students who refused to cooperate with the draft law proclaimed: "Time has brought us many lessons. The Abolitionist, the Suffragette, the union organizer—once lonely antagonists of entrenched customs—are today the undisputed victors in those very battles which in their day seemed lost beyond hope."[16]

Resisters were also assisted by veterans of the resistance movement during World War I. Under the terms of the 1940 Selective Service Act, all men between the ages of eighteen and sixty-five were required to register for the draft. COs from the earlier war found themselves eligible once again. Many remained firm in their anti-war ideals and helped give direction to the new generation of resisters.[17] Dr. Evan Thomas, the leader of the first work strike at Fort Leavenworth in 1918, became a public nonregistrant during World War II. Dr. Thomas had remained active in anti-draft organizing. He served as national chairman of the War Resisters League, as a member of the National Council of the Fellowship of Reconciliation, and as chairman of the New York Metropolitan Board of Conscientious Objectors.[18]

Julius Eichel was another World War I prison veteran active in resisting the later war. Eichel, an absolutist during World War I, organized a support group for the next generation of absolutists, the Absolutist War Objectors Association. He also helped publish an anti-draft publication, *The Absolutist*. Eichel's organization advocated complete noncooperation with the draft and urged imprisoned COs to participate in civil disobedience within the jails.[19] Roger Nash Baldwin also remained active in supporting COs. He chaired the American Civil Liberties Union committee on conscientious objectors.[20]

Cross-generational support for draft resisters has continued throughout every war and draft. Former resisters from World War II assisted Korean War resisters, and those from all three

wars helped Vietnam-era resisters. The modern anti-registration movement contains many former imprisoned COS in
leadership roles. In the book, *The Resistance*, two Vietnam-era
draft resistance leaders explain the importance of cross-generational support:

[They] offered more important help for the young men (and women)
who would create the new resistance: living examples of the possi-
bility of enduring loneliness, abuse and privation, and coming through
it creatively, and affirmatively. . . . For young men facing prison,
especially, such examples would be sources of strength.[21]

The resisters came from a broad variety of religious and political backgrounds. Although no complete index of the various religions and ideologies of conscientious objectors exists,
the Department of Justice put together a comprehensive
breakdown of the twelve major categories of imprisoned objectors: "religious," "moral," "economic," "political," "neurotic,"
"naturalistic," "professional pacifist," "philosophical," "socio-
logical," "internationalist," "personal," and "Jehovah's Witness."

The Justice report was ripe with unintended black humor.
It characterized the "neurotic" CO as someone who "has a
phobia of war's atrocities, a mental and physical fear and
abhorrence of killing and maiming, and who therefore cannot
participate in it." It described the "internationalist" as want-
ing to "destroy or abolish all international boundaries and
sovereignty, racial and trade lines, and consider the world one
big family of peoples devoid of war." The "professional pacifist" demanded "peace in our times at any cost. He would tol-
erate nothing which would inconvenience his mode of living. . . . He wants to enjoy all the protections of the
Government, but is unwilling to bear any of the responsibilities of citizenship." The "economic" resister believed that war
came from the "inequitable distribution of natural resources."
The "religious" objector took seriously the commandment, "Thou
shalt not kill."[22]

Although they came from many diverse backgrounds, militant COs shared a common faith in opposition to war. Con-

scientious objectors of almost every religious and political perspective published resistance statements, sometimes as letters to the public, and other times in small pamphlets or as statements to their local draft boards. In these declarations two themes appear again and again: the power of nonviolence and the individual's responsibility to make a personal choice regarding the morality of war. They express a belief that, regardless of how logical war appeared, how justified its ends, how righteous its causes—beneath these imperatives was human choice. No one had to choose war as a means of solving international problems. One objector put it this way:

[E]ach man as he sees the need to build a new world for man to live in will not be able to hide his expressions or emotions and will fight for what is right regardless of his past. We all live in this world until we make up our minds to build a new world. We then take a new hold on life with our hearts full of love for our fellow men and help show them the way.[23]

Many of the pacifists also believed that the war was going to fail. Even if the fascist armies were crushed, they maintained, world peace would not be won. Imperialism, colonialism, and other economic and political causes of the war would remain. As one resistance pamphlet eloquently stated:

Grapes can not be gathered from thorns.
Nor can figs from thistles.
Good ends are *not* achieved by evil means.
It is *not* possible to create a world of brotherhood
by hating and slaughtering our brothers.[24]

Although religious and personal expressions of faith in peace and nonviolence were basic themes running through the resisters' statements, many COs adopted specific rationales to support their own stance. One objector, Howard Schoenfeld, based his refusal to register for the draft on First Amendment grounds: "It legislates against conscience and political belief, which is in itself undemocratic, and it provides jail sentences for those who reject it on political grounds, as do the fascist laws of Germany, Russia, and Italy."[25] Another resister, Leon

Thomson, opposed the draft for political reasons. His arguments have the ring of contemporary protest against the large military budget:

We have a huge task in our country—to defend our civil liberties; to put our unemployed to work at productive labor; to put an end to the disabilities under which Negroes and other minorities suffer; to organize the vast resources and energies of this nation so as to provide the material basis of the good life for all our people.[26]

Regardless of the political climate generated by the war, the COs' deep commitment to nonviolence remained intact. The objectors' main contribution to world peace was not in assisting or halting World War II, but in keeping the pacifist ideal alive.

PRISON MISTREATMENT

Conscientious objectors suffered the deprivation and abuses of prison life. They faced strict prison routine, isolation or solitary confinement for punishment, a poor diet, boredom, and loneliness.[27] Unlike resisters from the previous war, the World War II objectors were tried in civilian courts and were not subjected to military courts-martial. The Selective Service System attempted to moderate the excessive brutality that had occurred during World War I. It stated its policy as one that attempted to "avoid the harsh treatment of COs, on the one hand, and their overly liberal treatment, on the other."[28] After sentencing, COs were confined in federal prisons, not military jails. The maximum sentence for violating the Selective Service Act was five years (the average resister served thirty-five months behind bars), not the ridiculously long sentences doled out at the World War I courts-martial.[29]

Despite the official policy against torture, a number of abuse cases were reported. In the West Street Federal House of Detention in New York City, an objector started a "protest scream" against the war. He was removed from his cell, placed in a barren isolation area, soaked with water, and left cold and wet throughout the night.[30] Also at West Street, a white objector refused to follow instructions that he sit at the all-white dining table. He preferred to sit with black inmates. In retaliation, he was placed in a tiny isolation subcell and beaten by a guard.[31]

At McNeil Island Federal Prison, a CO reported being beaten by guards. Other objectors were punished by denial of food, withholding of medicine, and the placement of objectors in cells with "sodomists and homosexuals with the obvious inference and implications."[32] In another prison a Molokan religious objector was placed in solitary confinement for 111 days and beaten "semi-conscious" for refusing to stop "discussing the Bible" with fellow inmates.[33]

The most unfortunate story to surface concerning a World War II objector was that of George Elder.[34] Elder was an indigent "hobo" of black and Native American descent. He was arrested in 1942 for "failing to notify his draft board of change of address." He was indicted and taken before a federal judge. According to Elder:

I was upset and angry. I told the judge I wasn't going to fight the Japanese. I said that it was Roosevelt's war. I told him I was a pacifist. I hated all wars, guns, riots, and violence. I was a conscientious objector. Why should I fight when this country treated the Indians so bad? I said the government should pay me $342.00 for my Indian rights.

The judge was infuriated by Elder's remarks and ordered him transferred to the Philadelphia General Hospital and later to the Byberry Mental Institution. In October 1942, a Byberry psychiatrist examined Elder and wrote:

Patient is intelligent . . . knows what is going on around him . . . converses freely in conversation . . . is coherent and relevant . . . patient is free of delusions and hallucinations. He is a conscientious objector. Exhibits persecutory trend. Is part Indian. Says government owes him money.

The diagnosis was "dementia praecox"—the inability to distinguish reality from illusion.

Elder was not released from Byberry until 1970 (twenty-eight years later), when he was sixty-three years old. He had no family or friends on the outside. He had become so accustomed to institutionalized living, it was reported, that he could not cope with his freedom. Within five months he went back to the institution.

A *cause célèbre* during World War II was that of Stanley Murphy and Louis Taylor. They were sentenced in 1943 to two and one-half years' imprisonment for walking out of a civilian alternative service work camp. When they entered prison in Danbury, Connecticut, both started a "fast unto death" to protest the war and the Selective Service. They fasted for eighty-two days before being transferred to the Prison Medical Center in Springfield, Missouri. At Springfield both Taylor and Murphy abandoned their hunger strike. Although clearly in need of hospitalization, they were thrown into a barbaric prison/insane asylum. Neither was accused of insanity. Both were beaten and placed in padded cells and "strip cells." Strip cells were barren, isolated units where inmates were kept naked and without blankets. A hole in the floor served as a toilet. Murphy and Taylor were able to smuggle letters out of Springfield documenting the pitiful conditions suffered by the general inmate population and outlining their own maltreatment. These exposures sparked a major investigation of the institution by the Department of Justice and called to public attention the abuse of mental patients.[35]

PRISON PROTESTS

From his unique perspective, James V. Bennet, the director of the Federal Bureau of Prisons during World War II, analyzed the results of incarcerating hundreds of well-educated, deeply religious, and politically experienced COs. He outlined numerous examples of prison protests and lamented:

[The objector is a] problem child—whether at home, at school or in prison. . . . Many members of this group come from respectable families and communities unaccustomed to the restrictions of prison life . . . to deal with a mother who speaks of prison officers as "the

lowest form of animal life" . . . or a propagandist who regularly re-
fers to the Bureau of Prisons as an agency of "ill-will," "torture" and
"brutality" requires grace.[36]

The objectors, much to the displeasure of the prison administration, continued the tradition of prison protests. All of these
protests were nonviolent, and some were extremely effective.

Although the majority of imprisoned objectors felt that their
obligations ended with opposing the draft, a vocal and active
minority protested the treatment of prisoners in federal jails.
They attacked a wide range of prison practices, including "Jim
Crow" (racial) segregation, censorship of prison mail, parole
practices, regimentation, and the excessive use of force.[37]

The major prison protests led by the objectors during World
War II were as follows:

Danbury, Connecticut. Between August 11 and December 23,
1943, twenty-three objectors participated in a work strike
against Jim Crow seating in the prison dining facility. White
and black inmates were forcibly kept apart in the dining hall
and other parts of the prison. Their 135-day strike succeeded,
making Danbury the first federal prison to desegregate its
dining facilities.[38]

Tucson, Arizona. In 1944, objector-led work and hunger
strikes led to improvements in food (less starch in diet); relax-
ation of letter censorship; and prison visits without the presence of guards.[39]

Tucson, Arizona. In late summer of 1945, a twenty-seven-
year-old CO, Manuel Tallis, went on a twelve-day hunger strike
against segregation in the prison dining facility. According to
press accounts, his efforts met with complete success.[40]

Milan, Michigan. Starting in 1942, individual and small
groups of COs initiated anti-Jim Crow strikes. Striking objectors lost "good-time" and were placed in isolation or transferred. Finally, the prison administration relented and allowed voluntary desegregation in the cell blocks and dining
room.[41]

Ashland, Kentucky. Fourteen inmates (twelve COs and two
regular inmates) refused to eat in the segregated dining hall.

The strike lasted six months, but failed when the protesters either were released from prison at the expiration of their sentences or were transferred to other institutions.[42]

Lewisberg, Pennsylvania. After a sixty-four-day hunger strike by six COs, prison officials granted demands concerning mail censorship, allowing *The Conscientious Objector* and *The Call* newspapers into the jail, and lessening the restrictions on books, diaries, and mail.[43]

In addition to collective action, a number of COs engaged in individual moral witness or protest behind bars. These actions were diverse and encompassed a range of activities from symbolic hunger strikes to complete noncooperation with jailers in every facet of prison life. These individuals caused the prison system considerable headaches. For example, Albon Man, a socialist objector, engaged in a hunger strike because the prison officials would not allow him to mail a letter.[44] Another objector, Milton Kramer, was considered "difficult to handle" because of his "extreme views" on "bi-racial" issues.[45] Kramer refused to donate blood because the Red Cross blood bank was racially segregated. In the presence of the warden, he handed the Red Cross doctor a protest note.[46] As punishment, Kramer was placed in isolation and deprived of 365 days of "good-time."[47] Losing his good-time effectively increased Kramer's sentence by one year.

Perhaps the most dramatic example of radical noncooperation with Selective Service rules was the Corbett Bishop case. Although he originally cooperated with the Selective Service and accepted assignment to a civilian public service camp, Bishop's opposition to the war intensified and he "walked out" of the camp in August 1944. This walk-out initiated a series of confrontations with the courts and prison officials which lasted until 1946, when the government abandoned its attempts to confine Bishop.

Every time Bishop was arrested, imprisoned, or forced to go into court, he would go completely limp, refusing to move or eat or talk with his captors. He engaged in complete noncooperation with every aspect of the system. Although sentenced to four years in jail for his walk-out, Bishop was released and rearrested three times. Each time he was rearrested, the prison system found it impossible to force-feed and maintain the noncooperating Bishop. In 1946, after a total of 426 days of complete passive resistance and fasting, the courts and prisons stopped prosecuting Bishop. He was released on parole, although he signed no parole papers and agreed to no parole conditions.[48]

Although the director of the Bureau of Prisons attacked the COs as products of "over-protective homes" and "mother fixations,"[49] the objectors had a significant impact on prison life, especially with regard to racial segregation.

CIVIL RIGHTS

A number of political and religious groups violated the draft law, not as pacifists but to express discontent with public policies not directly related to the war. Numerous individuals refused induction because the military practiced Jim Crow segregation. These young men refused induction as long as segregation existed; only if the army chose to desegregate would they join.

In 1945, George L. Haney, a twenty-nine-year-old black youth from Chicago, refused induction. After complying with all the Selective Service regulations and laws, Haney refused to take the oath of service. He told his draft board he would sign up only if the military desegregated: "Yes [I will sign]," he said, "provided that they send me to a branch of the service that will not discriminate against me because of my race."[50] At his trial, Haney was found guilty and sentenced to one year in jail. According to press accounts, the judge stated that imprisonment was necessary "to discourage other Negro objectors" from following Haney's course of action. The U.S. Attorney reportedly told Haney's counsel, [What would] the white people of the United States say if Haney had been freed?"[51]

In another Jim Crow case, Lewis Jones was sentenced to three years in Danbury for refusing to cooperate with the military because of discrimination against blacks. According to Jones' attorney, Jones was continuously denied parole in retaliation for his stand against racism:

There is no doubt whatsoever in my mind that the Parole Board is keeping this lad in because he is a Negro and has taken the stand he did. . . . Jones has made an excellent record . . . the whole case comes down solely to racial prejudice.[52]

Large numbers of Puerto Ricans refused draft induction to protest Puerto Rico's colonial status. The Puerto Rican nationalist movement claimed that Puerto Ricans were citizens of Puerto Rico and were not subject to U.S. draft laws. As early as 1940, young Puerto Rican men refused to register for the draft.[53] In 1945 it was reported that twenty-three Puerto Rican nationalists, four of whom were engaging in work strikes, were imprisoned at the Federal Correctional Institution in Tallahassee, Florida. The four strikers were placed in solitary confinement for forty days. While in solitary, the nationalists practiced complete noncooperation—one striker refused food for thirty days.[54]

Native Americans also refused to cooperate with the draft. Members of the Hopi Indian tribe announced their intention to refuse to register soon after the World War II draft law was passed. Pacifism had always played an important role in the Hopi religion. Many Hopis used draft resistance to protest the mistreatment of the American Indian. Riley Sunrise, a Hopi, wrote to his draft board:

Today my people, in common with the Indian race, stand in this so-called democracy branded in the movies, in most history books, and in the mind of the public generally as blood-thirsty savages with characteristics scarcely above that of the beast. We bear humiliating poverty, suffering and degradation. . . . I am not afraid to fight nor die . . . I merely object for the sake of the principle of Justice which is dearer to me than life.[55]

The U.S. Hopi Indian Agency condemned the Hopi resisters as "hostiles" and wrote the commissioner of Indian Affairs that these "insolent" resisters somehow thought they could refuse to "do something they did not want to do." The Hopis were ridiculed for believing that the jails "are for white men" and not for Indians.[56] Native Americans also used treaty law to justify resistance. But all attempts to claim that tribes were sovereign nations and exempted from supporting U.S. were rejected by the courts.[57]

Some Japanese-Americans incarcerated in relocation camps chose to violate draft laws. In the Heart Mountain Park relocation center in Wyoming, interned Japanese-American citizens formed a "Fair Play Committee" to test the constitutionality of the forced relocation of Japanese-Americans into concentration camps. The committee also initiated campaigns to improve the conditions within the camps. Soon after the committee was formed, a number of the leading officers received draft notices.[58] The Fair Play Committee held a mass meeting to protest the draft notices and unanimously passed a resolution endorsing draft resistance until the civil rights of all Japanese-American citizens were restored: "We, Members of the Fair Play Committee, hereby refuse to go to the physical examination or to the induction if or when we are called in order to contest the issue [of our confinement]."[59]

A total of sixty-three Japanese-American internees refused draft orders at the Wyoming camp. An FBI investigation revealed that the objectors were "loyal to the United States" and would join the military *if* their rights were restored.[60] In court the resisters argued that their forced removal into relocation camps was unjust and illegal, and that they had been removed from their homes and placed "behind barbed wire," without being charged with a crime.[61] They were found guilty of violating the Selective Service Act and sent to prison. On appeal, the U.S. Court of Appeals upheld their conviction. The appeals court judge reasoned: "Two wrongs never make a right.'[62]

CONCLUSION

Draft resistance did not collapse during World War II. Although resisters opposed the fascist armies, they were not willing to tone down their anti-war rhetoric, as did the Garrisonians during the Civil War. For the resisters, the "just" wars of the past had failed to achieve true social justice. The Civil War did not end racism, segregation, or the racial caste system. World War I did not succeed in "ending all wars." Violence, through injustice and war, remained a dominant theme in world affairs.

World War II resisters were convinced that war could not achieve peaceful world conditions. For them, violence had failed as a method of solving world tensions. World War II ushered in the nuclear era. Before the bodies were buried and the rubble cleared, the world was again on the brink of a new war. The Soviet Union and the United States were scrambling for spheres of influence in occupied Europe. The United States and its allies still sought to maintain the system of colonialism and exploitation of the Third World. Within three years of the end of World War II, the United States passed a new draft law, nearly identical to the 1940 law.[63]

NOTES

1. Henri Michel, *The Shadow War, Resistance in Europe 1939–1945*, 201-2; Werner Rings, *Life with the Enemy, Collaboration and Resistance in Hitler's Europe 1939–1945*, 185-88; Helen Fein, *Accounting for Genocide, National Responses to Jewish Victimization During the Holocaust*, 144-52; Gene Sharp, *The Politics of Nonviolent Action*, 189, 683.

2. Sharp, *Nonviolent Action*, 159-64; Michel, *Shadow War*, 202.

3. Sharp, *Nonviolent Action*, 314.

4. Ibid., 326.

5. Ibid.

6. Fein, *Accounting for Genocide*, 152-58.

7. Sharp, *Nonviolent Action*, 88, 189, 277, 313-14.

8. Fein, *Accounting for Genocide*, 141.

9. William L. Shirer, *The Rise and Fall of the Third Reich*, 294-95, 1269; Hannah Arendt, *Eichmann in Jerusalem: A Report on the Banality of Evil*; Fein, *Accounting for Genocide*, 121-42.

10. Selective Service System, *Conscientious Objectors Special Monograph No. 11*, 314-15.

11. Mulford Q. Sibley and Philip Jacob, *Conscription of Conscience: The American State and the Conscientious Objector, 1940–1947*, 31-35.

12. Selective Service System, *Conscientious Objectors*, 261.

13. Harry Elmer Barnes, article in *Prison World* (typescript, July 1944), Swarthmore Peace Collection (hereinafter SPC).

14. The Gara MID file is located in the National Archives in MID File No. 10902-169. All quotes are taken from this file.

15. Larry Gara, *War Resistance in Historical Perspective*; *Gara v. U.S.*, 340 U.S. 857 (1950).

16. *Why We Refused to Register*, 2, SPC.

17. Alfred Hassler, *Conscripts of Conscience*, SPC.

18. *WRL News*, July/August 1974, articles by Larry Gara and Julius Eichel.

19. Copies of *The Absolutist* are located at SPC; Hassler, *Conscripts*.

20. The work of Baldwin during World War II is fully documented in the World War II ACLU files regarding conscientious objectors. The ACLU papers are on microfilm at Brandeis University (hereinafter BU).

21. Michael Ferber and Staughton Lynd, *The Resistance*, 7.

22. Selective Service System, *Conscientious Objectors*, 3-4.

23. Henry Weber, letter of February 3, 1945, BU.

24. Hassler, *Conscripts*.

25. *Why We Refused to Register*, 1940, SPC.

26. Ibid., 3.

27. Sibley and Jacob, *Conscription of Conscience*, 352-72; author's interview with Ralph DiGia, New York, 1983.

28. Selective Service System, *Conscientious Objectors*, 1; Sibley and Jacob, *Conscription of Conscience*, 36.

29. Sibley and Jacob, *Conscription of Conscience*, 53.

30. *The Conscientious Objector* (hereinafter *The CO*), January 1944.

31. Ibid.

32. John Hampton, undated letter, reprinted in *The CO*, August 1945.

33. *The CO*, September 1943.

34. The Elder story is based on an article that appeared in the November 15, 1971, issue of *Win* magazine.

35. *The CO*, September 1943; May 1944; October 1944.

36. James Bennett, *Federal Prisons 1943, A Review of the Work of the Federal Bureau of Prisons During the Year Ending June 30, 1943*, 11, 13.

37. Sibley and Jacob, *Conscription of Conscience*, 372-78.

38. James Peck, *Underdogs vs. Upperdogs*, 68-83; Sibley and Jacob, *Conscription of Conscience*, 374.

39. *The CO*, April 1944.

40. *The CO*, October 1945; *The Los Angeles Times*, September 17, 1945.

41. *Chicago Defender*, February 2, 1946; CORE Press Release, July 21, 1945, BU.

42. John Mecartney, "Dear Friend" letter, July 23, 1945; Lewis Hill to Roger Baldwin letter, September 6, 1945, BU.

43. Ibid., January 1944; letter from strikers to Muste, January 23, 1943, BU.

44. *Grapevine*, February 1945, SPC.

45. James Bennett to Roger Baldwin, letter, October 31, 1944, BU.

46. Rev. E. Shurley Hognson, letter, November 29, 1944, BU. *Grapevine*, February 1945; *The CO*, April 1946.

47. Naida Axford, *Dear Friend* letter, November 6, 1944, BU. W. Osborne to A. J. Muste, *Memorandum of the National Service Board for Religious Objectors*, January 23, 1945, SPC.

48. Sibley and Jacob, *Conscription of Conscience*, 412-16.

49. Bennett, *Federal Prisons 1943*, 11, 12.

50. *Chicago Defender*, June 12, 1945.

51. Ibid.

52. *PM Magazine*, August 21, 1944; Clifford Foster letters, August 16, 1944, and March 21, 1944, BU; also see, *U.S. v. Downer*, 140 F.2d 397 (1944).

53. Women's International League for Peace and Freedom, letter to Baldwin, March 2, 1945, BU.

54. *El Imparcial*, March 17, 1945; Bennet to Baldwin letter (BU, March 2, 1945).

55. Riley Sunrise, letter to draft board, June 20, 1940, BU.

56. *New York Call*, April 23, 1945; Superintendent of Hopi Indian Agency to Commissioner of Indian Affairs, letter, December 24, 1940, BU; *Fellowship*, March 1945.

57. *Totus v. U.S.*, 39 F.Supp. 7, 9 (E.D. Wash. 1941); *Ex Parte Green*, 123 F.2d 862, 863 (2nd Cir. 1941); *Albany v. U.S.*, 152 F.2d 266 (2nd Cir. 1945).

58. *Kiyoshi Okamoto v. U.S.*, 152 F.2d 905, 906 (10th Cir. 1945).

59. Ibid.

60. *Shigeru Fujii v. U.S.*, 148 F.2d 298, 299 (10th Cir. 1945); *U.S. v. Fujii*, 55 F. Supp. 920, 930 (D.C. Wyoming 1944).

61. *Shigeru Fujii v. U.S.*, 148 F.2d at 299 (1945).

62. Ibid.; 65 S.Ct. 1406 (May 28, 1945). See also *Hideichi Takeguma v. U.S.*, 156 F.2d 437 (9th Cir. 1946).

63. Douglas McGregor, *Prosecutive Policy Under the Selective Training and Service Act of 1940—SS Circular No. 3421*, supplement no. 27, reprinted in Selective Service System, Special Monograph No. 14, 309.

5

The Draft and the Cold War

On March 17, 1948, President Harry S Truman addressed both houses of Congress and called for a resumption of the draft.[1] At the time, the President could not justify resumption with warnings of an imminent world war. Rather, Truman wanted to send a message to the world that America was willing to use its military power to achieve foreign policy objectives. Truman was clear about his intent: "The adoption of universal training [the draft] by the United States at this time would be unmistakable evidence to all the world of our determination to back the will to obtain peace with the strength for peace."[2]

This draft was fundamentally different from any other draft in American history, because the United States was neither on the brink of a world war nor actually engaged in major combat.[3] Truman designed the new draft to conscript young men into a large standing peacetime army. Its purpose was to insure adequate troops for America's growing military commitments, and to insure America's ability to engage in limited conventional wars, such as those destined to erupt in Korea, Vietnam, and the Dominican Republic. The Selective Service Act of 1948 was the draft law under which young men were inducted during both the Korean and Vietnam wars. The law is still on the books, and when President Jimmy Carter reintroduced draft registration in 1980, he used his powers under the original 1948 law.[4] In short, the 1948 draft was an integral part of the budding "Cold War."

The Cold War draft was not part of an emergency war crisis

where all people were asked to contribute or sacrifice in the name of democracy. Instead, the draft was becoming just another facet of American foreign policy. The congressional debates reflected these changes. Senator Chan Gurney, chairman of the Senate Armed Services Committee, said, "The committee is not here before you today with any contention that war is in the offing, nor even that it is inevitable."[5] Congressman Norris Cotton of New Hampshire supported the draft because he wanted "all the world to know" that the "peace-loving" United States maintained "strength and striking power."[6] Secretary of Defense James Forrestal testified before Congress that a draft was needed to provide "a strong (force), capable of striking sustained blows beyond the peripheral bases we now hold."

Confidential State Department and National Security Council memoranda pointed to a more insidious purpose for the Cold War draft. A top secret National Security Council memorandum, NSC-68, approved by the President in 1950,[7] spelled out a new role for American military policy in the post-World War II era: "Our overall policy at the present time may be described as one designed to foster a world environment in which the American economic system can survive and flourish."[8] NSC-68 explained that limited conventional war would be fought not only to deter Russian adventurism but also "to compel the acceptance of terms consistent with our objectives."

Planners sought an expansion of American military power to meet these new political and economic goals. For example, highly classified NSC documents, leaked during the Pentagon Papers scandal in the early 1970s, revealed the extent to which economic and political thinking stood behind America's escalating role in Vietnam. The documents highlighted the important place of Southeast Asia in America's new vison of world order:

Southeast Asia, especially Malaya and Indonesia, is the principal world source of natural rubber and tin, and a producer of petroleum and other strategically important commodities. The rice exports of Burma and Thailand are critically important to Malaya, Ceylon and Hong Kong.[9]

It was equally important that Southeast Asia not fall into the hands of the communists because of its economic significance for Japan:

The fall of Southeast Asia would underline the apparent economic advantages to Japan of association with the communist-dominated Asian sphere. Exclusion of Japan from trade with Southeast Asia would seriously affect the Japanese economy, and increase Japan's dependence on United States aid.[10]

Consequently, the NSC urged the government to "oppose any negotiated settlement with the Viet Minh" (Ho Chi Minh's forces)[11] in spite of the fact that the Viet Minh led the popular national liberation struggle against Japanese occupation during World War II.

Vietnam was not the only country affected by the new Cold War approach to international affairs. In the post-war era, American military or paramilitary forces were utilized in countries throughout the world, including Iran, Guatemala, Greece, Lebanon, Korea, and Cuba. The United States, either through direct military involvement or indirect covert operations by the CIA, intervened abroad "on the average of once every eighteen months either to bring down an unfriendly government . . . or to shore up a friendly one faced with insurrection."[12]

Future draftees would participate in military actions fundamentally different from those of the past. Conscripts would be used in police actions and limited wars with limited objectives. The change in the type of warfare in which conscripts were required to engage laid the foundation for the mass civil disobedience launched against the draft during the Vietnam conflict.

THE RESISTANCE RESPONDS

Cold War draft resistance began during the hysterical anti-communist "McCarthy era," a period when there was little tolerance for dissent from America's military policies. For example, the courts closed their doors tightly against religious

and moral justifications for violating registration laws or refusing to comply with orders from local draft boards. A stepfather who for religious reasons urged his stepson not to register for the draft was charged and convicted of violating the
Selective Service Act.[13] Although the young man registered for
the draft, his stepfather was nonetheless convicted of "advocating" nonregistration.

In another case, a newspaper editor was charged with
"knowingly counselling persons" to refuse to comply with the
draft laws. At her first trial, the court declared her insane and
confined her involuntarily in a mental institution.[14] Later, she
was tried and convicted on the Selective Service count. In up-
holding her conviction, the federal appeals court states: "[T]his
is a sad case where self-delusion has carried the defendant to
the point where she apparently believes her own warped ideas
of patriotism."[15]

Although draft resistance was minuscule during this period, the movement did not collapse under pressure from
McCarthyism. Resisters engaged in bold acts of public civil
disobedience. They called public attention to foreign policy alternatives to the Cold War, and they challenged the appearance of mass conformity engendered by the anti-communist
witch hunts.[16] As early as 1947, prior to the passage of the
1948 Selective Service Act, sixty-three New York City protesters took the bold and creative step of publicly burning their
draft cards.[17]

On April 2, 1948, a national "peacemakers" convention in
Chicago was attended by over 200 peace activists. Many leaders of the budding peace movement were present, including
formerly imprisoned COs Larry Gara, Julius Eichel, Jim Peck,
Ralph DiGia, Dave Dellinger, and Bayard Rustin.[18] Some of
these participants would play instrumental roles in the civil
rights and anti-war movements of the 1960s. Bayard Rustin,
for example, issued the call for the famous 1963 Civil Rights
March for Jobs and Freedom in Washington, D.C. Dave Dellinger became editor of the influential New Left magazine
Liberation and was later a defendant in the infamous "Chicago 7" trial.[19]

The peacemakers convention issued an unequivocal call for

civil disobedience against the draft: "It is not enough to speak, write, vote and send letters. . . . It is necessary to assume personal responsibility. . . . Therefore we refuse to bear arms. . . . [and] are unconditionally opposed to any form of conscription."[20] Collective and public acts against conscription were initiated. For example, the Peacemakers Society circulated a "We Say No!" petition. This petition asked potential resisters to put down their names as a public pledge not to cooperate with the Selective Service System. Over 200 people signed the illicit pledge.

The public acts were not intended primarily to undermine mass conscription; rather, they served the more important immediate function of making resisters aware that they were not alone in a sea of conformity. They were designed to shatter the illusion of complete public acceptance of the Cold War. The 1951 "We Say No!" petition stated:

The tendency toward universal registration and the urge to create an impression of uniformity and absence of protest are themselves manifestations of the trend toward totalitarianism to which we are opposed and against which the United States is ostensibly contending. We believe that it is best that the first time a person encounters a demand under a military conscription law, he should say NO.[21]

Similar "We Say No!" statements were successfully circulated throughout the course of the Vietnam War and appeared again during protests against the 1980 registration law.[22]

COLD WAR RESISTANCE AND KOREA

On May 4, 1949, William Heusel, a young resister from Nebraska, stood before a federal district court judge. Convicted of violating the Selective Service Act, he justified his actions by attacking America's role in the Cold War: "The 80th Congress was high-pressured into passing the Selective Service Act in the final rush before adjournment . . . the draft act resulted from fear, and it was designed to create fear in every potential enemy. As a way to peace and security, it is blind and stupid folly."[23]

The anti-draft movement started to redefine and enlarge its purpose. At first a strictly pacifist crusade, it became a campaign against Cold War interventionism. Conscientious objectors justified their actions by criticizing the government's policy toward the Third World. The doctrine of "containing communism" was ridiculed as a facade erected to hide greedy foreign expansionism. The peace activists advocated creative nonviolent alternatives to militarism.

A Peacemakers Society pamphlet condemned the Korean War as part of the Cold War folly:

[T]he Truman doctrine of containing Russia and Communism by force, no matter what name is applied to it and how good the motives of some who support it, means the attempt to set up an American Empire. . . . Uncle Sam, the exploiter and soldier, has to get out of Korea and the rest of the Orient. In order that Uncle Sam, the friend and the skilled worker, may enter.[24]

The opponents of the Korean War proposed policy alternatives to military intervention in the Third World. They attacked both Russian and American expansionism. Instead of supporting military intervention, the small anti-draft movement urged a policy of economic development. Colonial and imperial exploitation of the Third World must end, and poverty, illiteracy, and hunger must be fought. Moveover, the prospects of a prolonged Cold War and arms race between the United States and the Soviet Union horrified the resistance movement. They predicted a future of large standing armies, massive nuclear stockpiles, and continuous Cold War confrontation. To the anti-war movement, the Korean War symbolized this nightmare. A Fellowship of Reconciliation pamphlet read: "What Korea means . . . is that Russia and the United States are now engaged in an unlimited atomic and biological armaments race and are locked in a military power-struggle around the world."[25]

Some COs legally challenged the Korean War. In one case, James Bolton, a convicted resister, attacked his sentence on the grounds that the Korean War was an illegal "undeclared war." Although the court rejected his claim, his constitutional

challenge against the legality of waging undeclared wars became commonplace during the prolonged Vietnam conflict.[26]

THE CONTINUATION OF THE TRADITION

Despite changes during the Cold War period, draft resistance tactics developed in World War I remained at the foundation of the movement. Resisters continued to confront the
public with idealistic refutations of war. For example, Richard
Cameron, Jr., after being found guilty of refusing to register
for the draft in 1951, told the court: "Wars will continue at
least until all men refuse to cooperate with conscription. And
so for myself, I could not cooperate with the draft even if I were
exempted."[27]

Prison strikes led by conscientious objectors were reported
during the Cold War. In 1951, five COs at the Mill Point, West
Virginia, prison started to organize for the desegregation of the
prison. After a successful meeting of black inmates and white
COs, one of the white objectors was beaten unconscious by a
racist inmate. The five COs were then transferred to Ashland,
ending the desegregation campaign.[28] In another strike, four
COs at Springfield stopped work in symbolic protest of the
military system. In retaliation they were placed in the "hole"
and then in isolation for 85 consecutive days.[29]

Blacks and other minorities continued to resist conscription. When Congress was debating the new draft law, a group
of civil rights activists called for a national boycott of the Jim
Crow army. Led by civil rights and labor leader A. Philip Ran-
dolph and the newly formed Committee Against Jim Crow in
the Army, a wide range of civil rights leaders urged all youth
to refuse to comply with draft laws until the armed services
were desegregated. Congressman Adam Clayton Powell, Jr.,
and the National Association for the Advancement of Colored
People (NAACP) endorsed the boycott.[30] Black draft resisters
from World War II, such as Lewis Jones, who had refused to
join a Jim Crow army, were hailed by the black press.[31] The
movement had widespread support among blacks. One poll
showed that 71 percent of black college students supported the
boycott.[32] The political processes catalyzed by the boycott re-

sulted in President Truman's July 26, 1948, Executive Order
banning racial discrimination in the armed services.[33]

CONCLUSION

Despite McCarthyism and Cold War hysteria, draft resistance grew during the 1950s. Surprisingly, the percentage of
conscientious objectors grew to historical levels. In 1952, for
example, over ten times the percentage of inductees received
conscientious objector status than had even applied for objector exemptions during World War II. At that time, 0.14 percent of all inductees applied for objector exemptions. The
number of inductees gaining legal exemption grew almost every
year during the 1950s (Table 2). By 1960, the number of exempted objectors reached a startling 18.24 percent.[34]

During Korea and the Cold War, the draft resistance movement escalated. Two long-term forces caused this increase.

Table 2
Comparison of Conscientious Objector
Exemptions in World War I, World War II,
and Selected Cold War Years, 1952–1957

War/Year	Percentage of Inductees Exempted as Objectors
World War I	0.14
World War II	0.15
1952	1.64
1953	1.28
1954	3.63
1955	5.28
1956	9.17
1957	7.18

Source: Statistics extrapolated by the author from: Bureau of Prisons, *Annual Report,* 1949–1977;
Selective Service System, *Annual Report,* 1949–
1976; U.S. Bureau of Census, *Historical Statistics of the United States,* 1975; Selective Service System, *Conscientious Objectors Special
Monograph No. 11,* 53, 314–15.

First, the Cold War failed to generate the patriotism instilled by a national crisis. Second, thousands of draft-age youth participated in the growing civil rights movement.[35] These youths were inspired by the eloquent advocacy in support of civil disobedience by leaders such as Martin Luther King, Jr. Violating an "unjust" or "immoral" law, as a mechanism of social protest, became popularized. A new generation of conscientious objectors was violating the draft laws.

NOTES

1. *Congressional Record*, March 17, 1948, 2996.

2. *New York Times*, March 18, 1948; *Congressional Record*, ibid.

3. The draft laws of 1863 and 1917 were both passed *after* the Civil War and World War I, respectively, had been declared. The draft act of 1940 was passed while America stood on the brink of World War II and after France had been occupied by Germany. Franklin D. Roosevelt, *Registration Day Proclamation*, September 16, 1940. Even the U.S. court system took "judicial notice" that the Selective Service Act of 1948 was passed because of "the existence of the so-called 'cold war.' " U.S. Court of Appeals cited in Zelle Larson, *An Unbroken Witness*, 97.

4. Title 50 U.S.C. 450.

5. *New York Times*, June 3, 1948.

6. *Congressional Record*, 1948, A 4478; 2227.

7. NSC-68, cited in *Counterspy*, "Special Reprint No. 1," 2; NSC-68: A report to the National Security Council by the Executive Secretary on United States Objectives and Programs for National Security, April 14, 1950, cited in Walter LeFeber, *America, Russia, and the Cold War: 1945–1975*, 75-100 (hereinafter *Cold War*).

8. LeFeber, *Cold War*, 98-99.

9. *Statement of Policy by the N.S.C. on U.S. Objectives and Courses of Action with Respect to Southeast Asia*, reprinted in *The Pentagon Papers*, The Defense Department History of American Decision-making in Vietnam (Senator Gravel Edition), Vol. 1 (Documents), 385.

10. *NSC Staff Study on United States Objectives and Courses of Action with Respect to Communist Aggression in Southeast Asia*, February 13, 1952, reprinted in *The Pentagon Papers*, 375.

11. *NSC Staff Study*, 379.

12. Richard Barnet, *The Lean Years: Politics in the Age of Scarcity*, 220.

13. *Warren v. U.S.*, 177 F.2d 596 (10th Cir. 1949); see also *U.S. v. Henderson*, 180 F.2d 711 (7th Cir. 1950).

14. *U.S. v. Miller*, 131 F.Supp. 88 (D. Vermont 1955).

15. *U.S. v. Miller*, 233 F.2d 171 (2nd Cir. 1956).

16. Abraham J. Muste, *Of Holy Disobedience*, 30.

17. Michael Ferber and Staughton Lynd, *The Resistance*, 3.

18. *Peacemaker*, May 4, 1974.

19. *Who's Who in America*, 41st edition, Vol. 1, 843 and Vol. 2, 2868.

20. *Peacemaker*, April 7, 1973 (reprinting the "Call to a Conference").

21. *Peacemaker*, January 9, 1958.

22. "We Say No" statements reappeared in the 1980 anti-registration movement. See leaflet by National Resistance Committee, in author's files.

23. Statement of William Heusel (SPC, May 4, 1949).

24. *Peacemaker*, "Pacifists and the Korean Crisis" (SPC, July 25, 1950).

25. Fellowship of Reconciliation, *The Meaning of Korea* (SPC, 1950).

26. *U.S. v. Bolton*, 192 F.2d 805 (2nd Cir. 1951). Similar claims of illegality were rejected during the Vietnam War; see, for example, *Lutfig v. McNamara*, 373 F.2d 664 (D.C. Cir. 1967).

27. Richard Cameron, Jr., Statement (SPC, 1951).

28. *Peacemaker*, September 15, 1951; *NewsNotes*, September 1951; Larson, *An Unbroken Witness*, 120-21.

29. *Peacemaker*, July 21, 1951; Larson, *An Unbroken Witness*, 115.

30. *Congressional Record*, 1948, 4312-17.

31. Ibid., 4315.

32. Lawrence Wittner, *Rebels Against War, The American Peace Movement, 1941–1960*, 186.

33. Jack D. Foner, *Blacks and the Military in American History*, 182-85.

34. Extrapolation by the author from the following sources: Bureau of Prisons, *Annual Reports*, 1949–1977; Selective Service System, *Annual Reports*, 1949–1976; U.S. Bureau of Census, *Historical Statistics of the United States*, 1975; Selective Service System, *Special Monograph No. 11*, Vol. 1, "Conscientious Objectors," 314-15.

35. Ferber and Lynd, *The Resistance*, 10. See also Larson, *An Unbroken Witness*, 324. In her doctoral thesis Larson concluded that "the growth of absolutist sentiment among pacifists in the late 1940s and early 1950s undoubtedly bears upon the tremendous increase in acts of protest and defiance against conscription that we saw in the 1960s."

6

Vietnam and the Collapse of the Draft

In 1965 the U.S. Congress awakened to a growing anti-conscription movement. Its response was bipartisan and virtually unanimous: The movement had to be crushed. Senator John Stennis of Mississippi asked that the Department of Justice "immediately move to jerk this movement up by the roots and grind it to bits."[1] Senator William Proxmire of Wisconsin agreed with Stennis' call, and in a speech before the Senate he urged "vigorous and swift" prosecutions.[2] Senator Thomas H. Kuchel of California expressed outrage that "a few contemptible youths" had publicly destroyed their draft cards in his own state. The "infamous" anti-draft movement was "vicious, venomous, and vile," he said, and "replete with so-called conscientious objectors, beatniks."[3] Senate Majority Leader Michael Mansfield of Montana joined in: draft resisters, he said, "show a sense of utter irresponsibility and lack of respect . . . what these people have done is furnish fodder to Hanoi, Peiping and the Vietcong."[4]

Senator Frank J. Lausche of Ohio thought the movement was headed by "long-whiskered beatniks, dirty in clothes worn down, seemingly, by a willingness to look like a beatnik. . . . The point I am trying to make is that, substantially, these demonstrators are the project of communist leadership. Countless innocent, uninformed youth of the country are participating in them, not knowing that they are following the flag of the Reds and bowing to the voices of Communists dictating how they shall create disorder."[5] Senator Everett Dirkson of Illinois was so disturbed by the resisters that he pleaded with his colleagues: "[It's] enough to make any person loyal to his country weep . . . where in the name of conscience is their sense of history?"[6] Senator Richard B. Russell of Georgia blamed his Northern liberal colleagues for the upsurge in anti-draft activism:

I have said on the floor of the Senate that the fact that people in high places had encouraged campaigns of civil disobedience throughout this land in other cases [i.e. the civil rights movement] would bring home at other times under other conditions campaigns of civil disobedience that would be much more far-reaching and dangerous.[7]

Members of the House of Representatives expressed equal outrage.[8] Representatives Gerald Ford of Michigan [the future President] called the resisters "shameful and disgusting."[9] Representative Robert F. Sikes of FLorida commented:

[I]t was an extremely disagreeable thing to me to see the recent wave of demonstrations. . . . America has been shamed by the spectacle of organized treason and blatant cowardice . . . this sort of thing is encouraged by half-baked professors and communist sympathizers, as well as by professional agitators . . . crackpots who have little comprehension of world problems or American responsibilities.[10]

The draft resistance was coming of age.

The Vietnam War provided a catalyst for two trends that had been fermenting within the anti-draft movement—one tactical and the other ideological. Vietnam saw the advent of mass acts of civil disobedience coupled with a broadening of the ideological base of the resistance.

Abolitionists had attempted to generate mass civil disobedience to war, but their attempts failed. During World War I, World War II, and the Korean War, mass disobedience occurred on the first few days of conscription, but after that reaction waned, draft resistance again found its expression in individual, isolated acts. Draft law violation by its very nature is individualistic; each young person must make up his or her own mind about how to react. Once resistance is chosen, the path through the Selective Service System, the courts, and eventually jail can be very lonely. But the Vietnam War, with its mass public opposition, provided a radically different context for resisters. Public rallies against the war provided a perfect context for draft resisters to engage in collective civil disobedience. Draft boards were picketed, and draft cards often were publicly destroyed at major national demonstrations. Anti-draft activists, for the first time in history, engaged in sustained collective civil disobedience.

The second trend adding to the popularity of the resistance was ideological. Ever since the colonization of America, the philosophical base of draft resistance has been expanding. Early Quakers and other prerevolutionary resisters based their faith on deeply held religious convictions. Abolitionists politicized these religious beliefs but still advocated pure pacifism.[11]

In World War I, political objectors joined with religious objectors in violating the law. World War II witnessed the rise of various shades of anti-draft philosophies, such as those held by humanistic resisters, ethical resisters, civil rights resisters, and existentialist resisters. By the time the United States began drafting young men to fight in Vietnam, the base of the draft resistance movement had expanded far beyond the narrow pacifist and religious communities. It included political as well as moral opponents; it included those opposed to all wars and those opposed only to the Vietnam War.

THE RISE OF THE VIETNAM RESISTANCE: 1964–1965

In 1964, when the U.S. government escalated its involvement in the Vietnam War, a broad network of anti-draft organizations already existed, such as the War Resisters League, the Student Peace Union, Peacemakers, and the Committee for Nonviolent Action. In addition, an entire network of legal draft counseling services was available through organizations such as the American Friends Service Committee, the Central Committee for Conscientious Objectors, the National Interreligious Service Board for Conscientious Objectors, and a host of church-related counseling services.[12]

Many socialist parties also joined with the primarily pacifist-oriented networks in opposition to the draft. The "May

Second Movement" (M2M), a youth group associated with the
Progressive Labor party, circulated a "We Won't Go" pledge in
the spring of 1964. The pledge reflected the political platform
of the M2M and was clearly anti-imperialist in tone:

Believing that the United States participation in that war is for the
suppression of the Vietnamese struggle for national independence, we
see no justification for our involvement. . . . Believing that we should
not be asked to fight against the people of Viet Nam, we herewith
state our refusal to do so.[13]

In the summer of 1964, the DuBois Clubs, youth groups affil-
iated with the Communist Party of the United States, endorsed the M2M pledge and assisted in its circulation. By the
summer of 1965, more than one thousand students had signed
the "We Won't Go" pledge.[14]
    Other student-based organizations joined the draft resis-
tance agitation. The Student Nonviolent Coordinating Committee (SNCC), a civil rights group that had been in the forefront of the desegregation sit-in movement, issued a draft
resistance statement in 1965.[15] In addition, numerous cam-
pus organizations, such as the End the Draft (END), sprang
up across the country.[16]
    On April 17, 1965, the Students for a Democratic Society
(SDS) sponsored the first national demonstration against the
Vietnam War. SDS President Paul Potter, addressing the rally,
urged "massive civil disobedience" against the draft:

[W]e will build a movement that will find ways to support the increasing numbers of young men who are unwilling to and will not
fight in Vietnam; a movement that . . . will, if necessary, respond to
the administration's war effort with massive civil disobedience all over
the country, that will wrench the country into a confrontation with
the issues of the war.[17]

    Between 1964 and 1965, draft card burning became the "most
visible and controversial"[18] method of draft resistance. The
media widely covered the burnings and consequently popularized the tactic across the nation: "Draft card burning . . . became front-page news from coast to coast."[19] These burnings

symbolized public and collective resistance to the draft. The action brought resisters into the streets to commit civil disobedience against the Selective Service Act.

Congressional reaction to draft card burning was swift and hostile. In August 1965 Representative Mendel Rivers introduced legislation that made the destruction of a draft card illegal. The law passed both House and Senate by overwhelming margins, and President Lyndon Johnson signed the bill into law on August 30, 1965.[20] The law created a maximum sentence of five years for draft card burners. Although thousands of people would continue to burn their draft cards, only forty-six youths were indicted under this law, thirty-three of whom were convicted. Those prosecuted often were leaders of local resistance organizations.[21]

THE BIRTH OF MASS DISOBEDIENCE

In 1966 and 1967, grassroots support for draft resistance mushroomed. Small, locally based "We Won't Go" groups formed nationwide. Larger resistance organizations, such as CADRE (Chicago Area Draft Resisters), the New England Resistance, and the California-based Palo Alto Commune, provided national leadership to the growing youth movement. By the summer of 1967, an estimated sixty local "We Won't Go" groups had formed. These local anti-draft organizations and networks were broadly referred to as "The Resistance" and had organized thousands of young people.[22]

Opposition to the Vietnam War became a force uniting hundreds of local anti-draft groups. Regardless of local ideology—pacifist, socialist, religious, or "nonaligned"—the new anti-draft movement pulled together many diverse peoples. "We Say No" pledges became the most popular method of expressing draft resistance as part of the general resistance to the Vietnam War. One typical pledge, circulated by the San Francisco-based Committee for Draft Resistance, was signed by more than 800 people:

We, the undersigned, are compelled by the fundamental immorality and increasing brutality of our nation's course in Vietnam to now commit our lives to changing that course. We hereby urge and support open resistance to the draft and the military establishment which shapes and carries out this disastrous policy. . . . To all young men who are outraged by our nation's steps in Vietnam and who find it unthinkable and impossible to participate, we counsel, aid and abet their nonviolent refusal to cooperate with the military draft.[23]

Non-draft-age supporters also issued public statements supporting young draft resisters. The most famous of these was the "Call to Resist Illegitimate Authority," printed in the *New York Review of Books* on October 12, 1967. With more than 158 initial signatories, the "Call" urged illegal noncompliance with draft laws and pledged support to indicted resisters.[24] The Department of Justice indicted Dr. Benjamin Spock, Rev. William Sloane Coffin, Jr., Mitchell Goodman, Marcus Raskin, and Michael Ferber—all of whom had signed the Call and were leaders in the push for signatories. Although the conspiracy charges against them were eventually dropped, their defense campaign created a major national sensation. For example, more than 28,000 people signed statements "confessing guilt equal to that of the defendants."[25]

In the fall of 1967, the movement organized the most widespread mass civil disobedience in conscription history. A national "Stop the Draft Week" was called for the week of October 16. Rallies, pickets, and civil disobedience occurred at draft boards and induction centers across the United States, including New York City, Washington, D.C., Philadelphia, Minneapolis, San Francisco, Los Angeles, and Chicago.[26] In Washington, D.C., a delegation of national anti-war leaders handed one thousand returned draft cards to the Department of Justice and challenged the government to prosecute the resisters.[27] Later that week, during the national demonstration at the Pentagon (October 21-22), the "largest mass draft card burning" during the Vietnam conflict occurred, with uncounted hundreds of young men burning their draft cards.[28]

In Oakland, California, anti-war activists attempted to close down the Oakland induction center. An entire week of anti-draft actions was initiated by sending more than 300 draft cards to the local U.S. Attorney. The draft card turn-in was followed by a week of continuous pickets, sit-ins, and rallies at the induction center. Hundreds were arrested for committing civil disobedience, and picket lines around the induction center were often 10,000 strong. At times, more than twenty square city blocks were embroiled in confrontations between police and demonstrators, who attempted to close down the induction center.[29] In New York City more than 5,000 people demonstrated at the induction center, and 500 who committed civil disobedience were arrested.[30]

Resistance was no longer a purely solitary act. Although the ultimate decision to resist remained an individual's, the Vietnam protests created an atmosphere of collectivity. Mass civil disobedience paved the way for hundreds of thousands of young people to avoid induction both legally and illegally.

CIVIL RIGHTS RESISTANCE

As in World War II, national minorities used resistance to the draft law to call attention to the specific social and economic problems they faced.[31] The first black civil rights organization to oppose the draft was SNCC. In 1965 a SNCC chapter in McComb, Mississippi, issued a leaflet that read, in part:

No Mississippi Negroes should be fighting in Vietnam until the Negro people are free in Mississippi. . . . No one has a right to ask us to risk our lives and kill other colored people in Santo Domingo and Vietnam, so that the white American can get richer.[32]

Not surprisingly the SNCC resisters met with sharp and immediate rebuke. Within days of the SNCC statement's release, Mississippi Congressman Thomas Abernathy called for SNCC's suppression.[33]

Criticism was not limited to reactionary white Southerners. Charles Diggs, an influential black congressman from Detroit, attempted to dissociate war resistance from civil rights. Speaking in Congress, he said: "I think that our domestic problem is separate from any conflict that this country has with any other country. . . . Negroes have always been proud to have fought and died despite imperfections of this country."[34]

SNCC and other civil rights resisters faced harsh repression. In 1966, a small group of SNCC members picketed the Atlanta induction center. All were arrested. Six were sentenced to three and one-half years for "interfering with the administration of the Selective Service Act." Another picketer was sentenced to three years for "insurrection."[35]

Other civil rights organizations and leaders joined with SNCC in opposing the war. On April 6, 1967, Rev. Martin Luther King, Jr., came out against the Vietnam War on pacifist grounds. He urged all young people to seek exemption from the war by becoming conscientious objectors.[36] The backlash against King was vicious.[37] Both Northern civil rights leaders and Southern segregationists attacked King's stance. Representative O. C. Fisher of Texas claimed that King's anti-war position was a "crusade in favor of the communists in Vietnam." He called for King's indictment under the Selective Service Act, saying: "King has been both brazen and open in his violation of the law. And he is joined by more than a score of other sick minds and corrupt souls."[38] Along with SNCC and King, many other civil rights or black nationalist groups, including the Nation of Islam (Black Muslims),[39] the Congress on Racial Equality (CORE), the Black Panther party, and the Southern Christian Leadership Conference, adopted positions sympathetic to resistance.[40]

Blacks also challenged the discriminatory nature of the draft boards.[41] A 1967 government study revealed that minorities were systematically underrepresented on draft boards, with twenty-three states not having a single black board member.[42] (See Table 3). Blacks were overrepresented, however, in the armed services: they were drafted into the armed services at a rate almost twice as high as whites.[43] People from low-income backgrounds were twice as likely to perform combat duty in Vietnam than were people from middle- or high-income-level backgrounds.[44]

Legal attempts to end discrimination in the racial composition of draft boards failed. For example, Cleveland C. Sellers, a founder and national officer of SNCC, was indicted for resistance. Sellers challenged the legality of his all-white draft board's induction order. A military psychiatrist chastised Sel-

Table 3
**Survey of Black Draft Board Members in Ten Selected
States, 1966–1967**

State	Percentage Draft Board Members Black	Percentage State Population Black
Alabama	0.0	30.0
Arkansas	0.0	21.8
Florida	0.9	17.8
Georgia	0.2	28.5
Illinois	2.6	10.3
Louisiana	0.0	31.9
Mississippi	0.0	42.0
New Jersey	0.0	8.5
North Carolina	1.4	24.5
South Carolina	0.6	34.8

Source: National Advisory Commission on Selective Service, *In Pursuit of Equity: Who Serves When Not All Serve,* 80–81.

lers' involvement in the civil rights movement, calling him a "semi-professional race agitator."[45] The trial court rejected Sellers' claims. He received the maximum sentence, five years in prison.[46] The Supreme Court refused to hear Sellers' appeal and affirmed his conviction.[47]

In another draft case, a black defendant claimed that the chairman of his local all-white draft board was a member of the Ku Klux Klan (KKK). The court refused to allow questioning at the trial concerning the alleged KKK membership. The youth was subsequently convicted and sentenced to five years in prison.[48]

Throughout the 1950s and 1960s Puerto Rican nationalists continued to oppose conscription.[49] During the Vietnam era, the federal district court in Puerto Rico, however, became sympathetic to the nationalist cause. Significantly, Puerto Rico had no official representation in Congress and could not vote on conscription or support of the Vietnam War.[50] In a case involving leaders of the Puerto Rican nationalist movement, the federal judge felt compelled by the law to convict the resisters. But he publicly expressed his sympathy toward these "honest citizens"; he sentenced the nationalists to a mere "one hour" of confinement.[51] Indictments against nationalist resisters greatly diminished after this case.[52]

THE "ULTRA" RESISTANCE

The Selective Service System faced a completely new form of militant resistance during the late 1960s and early 1970s. Instead of violating the draft law and awaiting prosecution, adult opponents of the war broke into local draft boards in order to destroy draft records. Initially, the attacks were symbolic in nature. The protesters poured blood over files or burned them with napalm, and then remained on the scene for arrest by the police. The tactic was soon viewed not merely as symbolic, nonviolent protest, but as an effective hindrance to local Selective Service activity. The protesters would raid draft boards and attempt to destroy the records, thereby making it impossible for the board to call up inductees.[53]

The first such attack was led by Father Phillip Berrigan, a Jesuit priest, on October 27, 1967. Berrigan and three other anti-war religious resisters poured blood over draft files in Baltimore, Maryland. The next four years witnessed scores of similar attacks on draft boards.[54] (See Table 4). Initially, the arrested "ultra-resisters" were given long criminal sentences on such charges as "breaking and entering" and "destruction of government property." But as the number of actions grew, and the war continued, the ultra-resisters received shorter or suspended sentences. One group arrested while breaking into a draft board was found not guilty by a sympathetic jury. The jurors were swayed by evidence of government misconduct and the immorality of the Vietnam War.[55]

PRISON RESISTANCE

Vietnam resisters continued the tradition of prison agitation begun by draft resisters in World War I and World War II. Imprisoned Vietnam COs worked hand-in-hand with the general inmate population in protesting a wide range of grievances, including prison "slave labor," mail censorship, poor food,

Table 4
Selected Breakdown of Destroyed Selective Service Records, 1968–1971

Date	City	Number Destroyed
5/68	Catonville, Md.	378
6/68	Boston, Mass.	"Several hundred"
9/68	Milwaukee, Wis.	20,000
5/69	Pasadena, Calif.	500
5/69	Silver Spring, Md.	"Several hundred"
5/69	Chicago, Ill.	20,000
7/69	New York, N.Y.	"Several thousand"
8/69	Bronx, N.Y.	75,000
8/69	Queens, N.Y.	"Several thousand"
9/69	Akron, Oh.	100,000
10/69	Indianapolis, Ind.	44 Draft boards
11/69	Boston, Mass.	100,000
6/70	Providence, R.I.	All 1-A files of 4 boards
12/70	Philadelphia, Penn.	"Thousands"
4/71	Evanston, Il.	300–500

Source: Extrapolated by the author from: Michael Ferber, *The Resistance*, 201–21; Jerry Elmer, unpublished manuscript (1980); *Peacemaker*, May 22, 1971, and July 7, 1973; Lawrence M. Biskir and William A. Strauss, *Chance and Circumstance: The Draft, the War and the Vietnam Generation*, 66–67.

arbitrary parole procedures, abusive psychiatric practices, unsanitary hospital conditions, racial discrimination, arbitrary transfer policies, and poor educational facilities. A partial list of the major prison strikes and protest actions which COs organized or participated in includes:

Texarkana, Texas, May 1972. Approximately 90 percent of the inmates participated in a three-day work strike over prison conditions, including the lack of educational facilities and the low prison wages. A draft resister was accused of leading the strike, placed in isolation, and threatened with additional criminal charges, for example, "inciting mutiny among the inmate population."[56]

Marion, Ohio, February 1972. Prisoners began a nonviolent work strike, and they presented fifteen demands to the prison administration. As a result, the prison was sealed off from the outside, and the inmates were placed in lock-up.[57]

Lewisberg, Pennsylvania, February 1972. Five hundred of Lewisberg's 1,400 inmates engaged in a work strike. The administration agreed to negotiate with an inmate committee.[58]

Petersburg, Virginia, April 1973. An unspecified number of inmates went on a work strike. They demanded better food, medical attention and jobs, and an end to religious discrimination. Authorities reported that the strike was "subdued" when the "so-called organizers were placed in segregation and later transferred to various federal prisons."[59]

Terre Haute, Indiana, November 1972. Approximately 70 to 80 percent of the prison population engaged in a work strike to protest parole practices, lack of educational opportunities, and low prison wages.[60]

La Tuna, Texas, August 1971. Almost 90 percent of a prison population of 700 went on strike, primarily over discrimination against Chicano inmates. The warden agreed to negotiate with an elected inmate council. He also agreed not to transfer or discipline any of the striking inmates. The prisoners returned to work.[61]

Allenwood, Pennsylvania, January 1969. Twelve resisters went on a work strike demanding recognition of an elected inmate council. All of the strikers were transferred to Lewisburg.[62]

Danbury, Connecticut, February-March 1972. The entire prison population participated in a general work strike. The administration promised to compromise. Fearing retaliation, a majority of the inmates went back to work. Those who refused to return to work were punished, placed in isolation, and deprived of "good-time."[63]

Individual Resistance. Imprisoned COs engaged in numerous acts of absolutist noncooperation and individual protest actions. When one resister went on a strike, he was placed in the "hole" for refusing to perform unpaid prison "slave labor."[64] A number of prisoners fasted to protest the war and prison conditions. Although one can only estimate the number of individual fasts or hunger strikes, in 1972 alone fasts were reported in prisons in Lewisburg, Springfield, and Danbury.[65]

One of the unique actions organized by jailed resisters was a "conference on nonviolence" at the El Reno federal prison. Veteran resister Larry Gara wrote enthusiastically about its potential: "The conference, which was viewed skeptically by many prisoners, attracted a large number at each session, ending with an arm-around-your-neighbor circle which even included the warden. Visitors and prisoners contributed ideas, music and role playing."[66]

THE COLLAPSE OF CONSCRIPTION

Although there were dramatic incidents of mass public civil disobedience against the draft, most anti-war COs resisted the draft as individuals or as members of very small local communities. Essentially, no national program or national anti-draft organization existed. The movement was grassroots in style and almost anarchistic in structure.

The local activities of resisters varied.[67] Some resisters and their supporters operated draft counseling services, others picketed Selective Service offices, and still others formed committees to support the criminal defense of a local resister. Many resisters organized teach-ins, sit-ins, and public draft card turn-ins. Many local churches and attorneys offered legal services to draft-age youth. Both the National Lawyers Guild and the National Emergency Civil Liberties Committee provided attorneys to aid indicted resisters.[68]

These grassroots projects worked hand-in-hand with national events. When the United States invaded Cambodia in May 1970, protesting students were shot dead at Kent and Jackson State Universities. Massive nationwide anti-draft activities followed the killings. Within weeks, more than 10,000 draft cards were returned, and anti-draft pledges were signed and sent to government officials. By November 1970, that number had risen to 25,000.[69]

By the early 1970s, the Selective Service System was in deep trouble. Public demonstration and attacks on local draft boards

had made it difficult for the Selective Service to rent space:
"Trying to find new quarters, GSA [General Services Admin-
istration] learned that owners of single-tenancy property would
not lease to them because they had been threatened with in-
surance cancellation if their property was occupied by a draft
board."[70] The Selective Service's staff became demoralized. Staff
turnover rates increased 300 percent between 1965 and 1968—
rising from just over 6 percent per annum to more than 18
percent.[71] An article in *New York Magazine* in June 1970
summed up the problems facing draft offices around the country:

Draft resistance in New York City has become so widespread and so
sophisticated that the Selective Service System, cumbersome to be-
gin with, today seems barely capable of drafting anyone who doesn't
care to be drafted. . . . [The office] is now lumbering along, con-
fused, demoralized, and ineffectual in the face of the new resistance.[72]

The Criminal Division of the Department of Justice complained publicly of the difficulty it had in convicting COs. William S. Sessions, the chief of the Government Operations Section of Justice's Criminal Division, testified before the House
Armed Services Special Subcommittee on the Draft:

Organizations throughout the nation are openly advocating defiance
of the draft law . . . such activities seem to present nearly insurmountable obstacles to prosecution. Counselors invariably are careful to couch their speeches in contexts of protest against the war so
as to come within the First Amendment protection.[73]

By November 1970, the director of Selective Service predicted that the draft was doomed. The conservative news
magazine *Human Events* reported that the director "stated last
November that the draft had become so unpopular it was living on borrowed time, and that Congress might soon eliminate the President's power to conscript men for military service."[74]

CONSCIENCE AND THE JUDGES

Prior to the Vietnam War, it was a maxim that "conviction is almost inevitable" in Selective Service Act cases.[75] Under the provisions of the Selective Service Act, issues of conscience need not be argued before a jury. When an objector refuses to cooperate with his local draft board, he faces prosecution by the Department of Justice. The only question examined at his subsequent criminal trial is: Did the young man in fact register for the draft, or did the young man refuse to report for induction? Such issues of fact are seldom in dispute. The resister is usually willing to admit that he refused to register or report for induction. But most resisters seek an opportunity to explain to the jury their reasons for violating the draft law.[76]

The controversial issues in a draft case—such as the reasons a resister opposes war or refuses to cooperate with the draft law—are not usually argued before the jury. The Supreme Court held that issues of conscience are only to be decided by the local draft board or the Selective Service appeals board. (This is true despite the fact that the draft and appeals boards are appointed and accountable to the President and must fill monthly quotas of inductees.)[77] In *Cox v. United States*, the Supreme Court held that "the constitutional right to a jury trial does not include the right to have a jury pass on the validity of an administrative order (i.e. the determination of the Selective Service's local draft and appeals boards)."[78] In subsequent cases, the Supreme Court has held that the legal or religious objections of a CO, the illegality of a war, and even the proven error of a local draft board need not be argued before a jury. The issue can remain narrow and simplistic. The objector has no judicially recognized legal right to present an anti-war or a pacifist defense.[79]

At the beginning of the Vietnam War, the federal judiciary reacted as it had during other wars—with judicial conservatism and outright hostility to the resistance position. In 1967, the conviction rate in Selective Service Act cases was 75 percent. Of those convicted, 89 percent were sentenced to jail, with an average sentence of thirty-two months.[80] In many early cases, judges referred to resisters as "dangerous criminals" who were "attempting to overthrow the government."[81]

In a 1965 case, for example, David H. Mitchell III was indicted for failure to report for induction. At trial he attempted to challenge the legality of the Vietnam War, calling it an illegal war of aggression, a violation of international law, and a violation of the Nuremberg war crimes treaties.[82] The federal district court judge rejected these claims, labeling them "degenerate subversion." He called Mitchell a "sickening spectacle" who "seize[d] the sanctuary" of freedom of speech to assert "tommyrot."[83] Mitchell was convicted and sentenced to the maximum term of five years in prison.[84]

Even in the face of vindictiveness, resisters persisted in their attempts to persuade judges of the righteousness of their cause. The statement of Jim Wilson, a convicted religious objector, is typical of the confrontations that occurred regularly at draft law trials:

I stand in this court as a Roman Catholic . . . a believer in the teachings of Jesus Christ. . . . I stand accused of committing the so-called crime of refusing to be inducted into the armed forces. I plead guilty to this charge because that is exactly what I have done: refused to be inducted into an institution that orders and trains men to kill. You may ask . . . why I have not applied for the status of conscientious objector if I feel this way? The only answer that I can honestly give is that I cannot cooperate in any way with the system of conscription.[85]

The trial judge ridiculed Wilson for being "immature" and "arrogant."[86]

In another case, a convicted CO wrote to his sentencing judge from prison. In his letter he pleaded with the judge to join the ranks of the anti-war movement:

There comes a time in all our lives when we must decide between right and wrong. We all have to learn when to do as we are told, and when to do what is right. . . . We must learn to draw lines, and be strong enough to stand by them under pressure. I draw my line short of supporting senseless and brutal mass murder. Where and when will you as a man draw yours? You and your colleagues are in an excellent position to help end this misery. By handing out acquittals to draft-related offenders, you could render ineffective one of the tentacles of the monster.[87]

Draft resisters were bringing conscience into the courts.

During the more popular wars, court decisions reflected the patriotic mood of the general population. Objectors' stand were viewed as treason or political insanity. Anti-war appeals to conscience failed. But conscription for the Vietnam War was part of the Cold War draft. It was designed to conscript soldiers for an unpopular conflict, not to protect the United States from invasion. Eventually, draft resisters succeeded in bringing conscience into the courts.

As opposition to the war and the draft mounted, the judicial system responded with increasing flexibility. Between 1967 and 1975, the percentage of defendants convicted of Selective Service Act violations dropped every year. Similarly, the average sentence of those convicted dropped almost every year. In 1967, for example, three-fourths of all Selective Service Act defendants were convicted. That proportion declined almost every year. By 1970, the conviction rate had fallen to just over 36 percent. By 1975, less than 17 percent of all draft law defendants were convicted.[88] (See Table 5.)

Startling drops in the percentage of convicted resisters given jail terms coincided with the drop in the conviction rate. In 1967, nearly 90 percent of all those convicted of draft law crimes received jail terms; that proportion had been cut in half by 1970. By 1975, less than 9 percent of all convicted defendants went to prison.[89] For those sentenced to prison, the average length of their sentences also dropped, from a high of a 37.3 months in 1968 to a low of a 14.5 months in 1974.[90] (See Table 6.)

Both the drop in conviction and imprisonment rates and the decline in the average length of prison sentences are indicative of changing judicial attitudes. Draft resisters were viewed less and less as dangerous un-Americans or immature fanatics. Some judges praised the courage of resisters and compared their determination and tactics with other great civil disobedience crusades, such as the Gandhian movement for Indian independence. On May 19, 1972, for example, five war

Table 5
Conviction Rate for Vietnam-Era
Draft Law Violators, 1966–1975

Year	Convictions as a Percentage of Indictments
1966	72.0
1967	75.1
1968	65.8
1969	51.6
1970	36.3
1971	34.8
1972	33.5
1973	28.0
1974	38.2
1975	16.6

Source: Extrapolations from *Federal Offenders in U.S. District Courts,* Administrative Office of the United States Courts, cited in Lawrence M. Biskir and William A. Strauss, *Reconciliation After Vietnam: A Program of Relief for Vietnam-Era Draft and Military Offenders,* 132.

resisters who had raided the draft board in Buffalo, New York, were convicted of "conspiracy and intent to commit burglary." They faced up to twelve years in prison. Federal District Court Judge John T. Curtin suspended the defendants' sentences. He called the Vietnam War a "horror" and praised the courage displayed by the defendants:

If I may interject at this moment, it seems to me that there may be a strong argument made that the time spent, the efforts spent by you, and action taken, would indicate that your love of country is above that of most all other citizens because you had the moral outrage to put into action what you believe. If people had the same sense of morality as you did, it would seem to me that the war would have been over a long time ago.[91]

Table 6
Percentage of Draft Law Violators Sentenced to Jail and
Average Length of Sentence of Those Imprisoned, 1967–1975

Year	Percent Given Prison Time	Average Length of Sentence of Those Imprisoned (months)
1967	89.2	32.1
1968	73.9	37.3
1969	60.4	36.3
1970	43.8	33.5
1971	36.3	29.1
1972	27.8	22.0
1973	26.6	17.5
1974	19.3	14.5
1975	8.7	no number cited

Source: Extrapolations from: *Federal Offenders in U.S. District Courts,* Administrative Office of the United States Courts, cited in Lawrence M. Biskir and William A. Strauss, *Reconciliation After Vietnam: A Program of Relief for Vietnam-Era Draft and Military Offenders,* 130, 132.

Perhaps the most dramatic acquittal of war resisters came at the trial of twenty-eight anti-war activists in Camden, New Jersey. The "Camden 28" were caught breaking into the local draft board. Each faced a maximum sentence of forty-seven years in prison and fines of up to $46,000 for "seven counts of breaking and entering, stealing files, destroying files, damaging government property, interfering with the administration of the Selective Service Act, possessing burgulary tools and conspiracy."[92] The defendants admitted to the jury that they had done everything they were charged with. But they pleaded with the jury to acquit them anyway.

Their defense was based on police misconduct. One of the major planners of the action was an FBI informer. The informer had helped plan the draft board raid and insured that the police arrested the defendants when they attempted to break into the office. They also based their defense on moral opposition to the Vietnam War. According to reports of the trial in the *New York Times*, defense attorneys asked the jury to "ignore the laws against breaking and entering and to acquit them as a means of saying that the country had had enough of the 'illegal and immoral' war in Vietnam."[93] The jury voted unanimously to acquit the defendants on all counts.[94]

After the trial, one juror, Mrs. Anna Bertino, a widow and a small business owner, said that "there was a strong feeling among the jurors that they wanted to join the defendants in taking a stand against the war."[95] Another juror, Samuel Braithwaite, an Atlantic City cab driver, wrote a note to the defendants at the end of the trial:

Well done for trying to heal sick, irresponsible men who were chosen by the people to govern and lead them . . . men who failed people by raining death and destruction on a hapless country. To you [the defendants] . . . for your God given talents, I say "well done!"[96]

INDUCTION BREAKDOWN

By the end of the Vietnam War, both legal and illegal draft resistance had seriously undermined the ability of the Selective Service to induct large numbers of young men into the armed services. In 1970, a quarter of all inductees were granted objector status; in 1971, that proportion had increased to more than 42 percent. Toward the end of the Vietnam War, CO exemptions reached previously unthinkable proportions. By 1972, more young men were exempted from the draft than were inducted into the armed services.[97] (See Table 7.)

The number of criminal defendants also soared during the Vietnam War. Between 1965 and 1975, 22,467 young men were indicted for draft law violations; of those, 8,756 were convicted and 4,001 were imprisoned.[98] The overwhelming majority of those convicted of violating the Selective Service Act were motivated by "anti-war" sentiments. For the first time in history, religious objectors were a minority of those convicted: 72 percent of the convicted were either nonreligious or members of a nonpacifist church. Only 7 percent of the convicted re-

Table 7
**Legal Conscientious Objector Exemptions in the
Vietnam Period in Comparison to World War I
and World War II Rates**

War/Year	Ratio of Objector Exemptions to Actual Inductions (per 100 Inductions)
World War I	0.14
World War II	0.15
1966	6.10
1967	8.11
1968	8.50
1969	13.45
1970	25.55
1971	42.62
1972	130.72
1973	73.30

Source: Statistics extrapolated by the author from: Bureau of
Prisons, *Annual Report,* 1949–1977; Selective Service System, *Annual Report,* 1949–1976; U.S. Bureau of Census, *Historical Statistics of the United
States* (1975); Selective Service System, *Conscientious Objectors Special Monograph No. 11,* 53, 314–
15.

sisters came from traditional pacifist religions, whereas the
remaining 21 percent were Jehovah's Witnesses.[99]

As the war continued, the percentage of youth willing to face
prosecution also rose. Criminal defendants comprised a mere
0.015 percent and 0.012 percent of all inductees during World
Wars I and II, respectively. During the Vietnam conflict this
percentage grew by astronomical proportions. By 1972, an unprecedented 12 percent of all inductees were indicted; this is
an increase of more than 1,000 percent over the earlier rates.
A young man facing induction during the Vietnam War was
thus one thousand times more likely to resist the draft and be
indicted than were his counterparts during prior wars.[100]

By the end of the Vietnam War, the Selective Service System was demoralized and frustrated. It was increasingly dif-

ficult to induct men into the army. There was more and more illegal resistance, and the popularity of resistance was rising. The draft was all but dead.

THE END OF THE DRAFT

In December 1972, President Richard M. Nixon ended all draft calls.[101] For the first time since 1948 no young men were conscripted into the armed forces. The longest standing draft in American history had come to an end. In 1975 President Gerald R. Ford issued a proclamation terminating the remaining draft registration requirement.

The nation had turned around. Most of the fierce red-baiting of resisters had ended. The war had been discredited, and the resisters vindicated. Instead of being attacked on Capitol Hill, draft resisters were being praised. House member Parren J. Mitchell, for example, thanked the resisters for helping change public opinion on the war and draft:

[P]unishment and ostracism of draft dodgers and deserters will not stop the process of moral examination of the government's law. It will never assure blind obedience, thank God. As long as there are thinking people, there is going to be resistance to war. The results of the resistance to the Vietnam war were that the entire nation finally coalesced in a united demand that we "get out of Vietnam." This outcry for peace was largely brought about by the efforts of the young men who dared to dissent. We should laud those young men for their role in the establishment of peace.[102]

Other representatives recognized the importance of the anti-draft movement in changing America's opinion on the war. Congresswoman Bella Abzug of New York said:

They have paid the price for following the moral imperative: Thou shalt not kill. They were among the first to challenge the morality of our acts in Vietnam. They made us think more deeply about what we were doing there. The courage of this lonely stand is hard to imagine.[103]

In 1977 the newly elected President Jimmy Carter pardoned all of the people convicted of violating the Selective Service Act during the Vietnam period.[104] The Cold War draft had died.

Resistance to the draft during the Vietnam era came close to the realization of a dream. The resistance may not have ushered in a revolutionary pacifist epoch, but it did end the longest draft in American history and help alter America's interventionist foreign policy.

All the traditions, ideologies, and tactics of war resistance came together during Vietnam. The small groups of absolutist resisters that confronted the draft during every war in American history grew into a mass public civil disobedience movement. Religious ideals against killing were joined with pacifist and pragmatic politics. The weak ideological underpinnings of the Cold War draft tore the Selective Service System apart. That draft, once rendered ineffective, was ultimately discredited. War as a foundation for American international relations was dealt a blow.

But the movement did not put an end to militarism. The conscript army was replaced by a volunteer army. The nuclear arms race escalated, and the interventionist option for Pentagon planners continued as a viable alternative to peaceful negotiation and détente. Seven years after the end of the Cold War draft, President Carter reintroduced draft registration. The very contradictions remaining after Vietnam allowed the same President who pardoned the old resisters to create a new generation of draft resisters.

NOTES

1. *New York Times*, October 16, 1965.
2. *Congressional Record*, October 18, 1965, 27252.
3. Ibid., 27251.
4. Ibid., 27252.
5. Ibid., 27253.
6. Ibid., 27254.
7. Ibid., 27253.
8. Ibid., October 21, 1965, 27895.
9. Ibid., October 20, 1965, 27425.
10. Ibid., 27724.

11. Michael Ferber and Staughton Lynd, *The Resistance*, 50-51; *Peacemaker*, May 1964.

12. Ferber and Lynd, *The Resistance*, 136.

13. The Progressive Labor party and the M2M altered their position on the draft in 1965. Instead of urging draft resistance, they called on their members to join the military and agitate among the enlisted men. Ibid., 136.

14. Fred Halstead, *Out Now! A Participant's Account of the American Movement Against the Vietnam War*, 163.

15. Ferber and Lynd, *The Resistance*, 31.

16. Ibid., 17.

17. Ibid., 34.

18. Ibid., 21.

19. Ibid., 21.

20. Ibid., 22.

21. Lawrence M. Biskir and William A. Strauss, *Reconciliation After Vietnam: A Program of Relief for Vietnam-Era Draft and Military Offenders*, 85. *U.S. v. O'Brien*, 391 U.S. 367 (1968); *U.S. v. Smith*, 249 F.Supp. 515 (S.D. Iowa 1966); *U.S. v. Rehfield*, 416 F.2d 273 (1969).

22. Ferber and Lynd, *The Resistance*, 50, 64.

23. Ibid., 120.

24. Ibid., 121-25.

25. Ibid., 124; see also *U.S. v. Spock*, 416 F.2d 165 (1st Cir. 1969).

26. Michael Useem, *Conscription, Protest, and Social Change*, 3.

27. Halstead, *Out Now*, 345.

28. Ferber and Lynd, *The Resistance*, 136.

29. Halstead, *Out Now*, 344-45.

30. Ibid., 352-53.

31. There were numerous unsuccessful attempts by Native Americans to use treaty law to claim exemption from the armed services. See, for example, *U.S. v. Rosebear*, 500 F.2d 1102 (8th Cir. 1974); *Williams v. U.S.*, 406 F.2d 704 (9th Cir. 1969); *U.S. v. Neptune*, 337 F.Supp. 1028 (D. Conn. 1972); see also *The Movement*, October 1967.

32. *Congressional Record*, August 3, 1965, part 14; Ferber and Lynd, *The Resistance*, 31.

33. *Congressional Record*, August 3, 1965, 19243.

34. Ibid.

35. Ferber and Lynd, *The Resistance*, 33; see also *U.S. v. Lewis*, 275 F.Supp. 1013 (E.D. Wis. 1967).

36. *New York Times*, April 15, 1967.

37. Michael Harrington, *Washington Post*, April 16, 1967, "Style Section," 1.

38. *Congressional Record*, May 9, 1967, 12204.

39. Many adherents of the Nation of Islam, including famous boxer Mohammed Ali, refused induction into the army. Some, like Ali, received legal CO exemptions. Many others were denied legal exemptions and imprisoned. See, for example, *Clay v. U.S.*, 403 U.S. 698 (1971); *Joseph v. U.S.*, 405 U.S. 1006 (1972); *U.S. v. Mohammed*, 288 F.2d 236 (7th Cir. 1961).

40. *New York Times*, January 19, 1967; February 18, 1967; April 5, 1967; May 21, 1967; June 28, 1967; July 24, 1967; January 9, 1968.

41. National Advisory Commission on Selective Service, *In Pursuit of Equity: Who Serves When Not all Serve?*, 80-1.

42. Ibid.

43. American Friends Service Committee, *The Draft, Its Impact on Poor and Third World Communities*.

44. Ibid., citing Lawrence M. Biskir and William A. Strauss, *Chance and Circumstance: The Draft, the War and the Vietnam Generation*, 9.

45. *Sellers v. Laird*, 395 U.S. 950, 953 n. 5 (1969).

46. *Congressional Record*, July 7, 1971, 25651.

47. *Sellers v. Laird*, 395 U.S. 953.

48. *DuVernay v. U.S.*, 394 F.2d 979, 980 (5th Cir. 1968).

49. *Alicia Ruiz v. U.S.*, 180 F.2d 870 (1st. Cir. 1950); *U.S. v. Valentine*, 288 F.Supp. 957 (D. Puerto Rico 1968); *U.S. v. Vargas*, 370 F.Sup. 908 (D. Puerto Rico 1974).

50. *Valentine*, 1294.

51. *U.S. v. Feliciano-Grafals*, 309 F.Supp. 1292, 1294, 1300-1301 (D. Puerto Rico 1970).

52. *Peacemaker*, February 22, 1969; *New York Times*, April 6, 1967; *San Juan Star*, November 14, 1967.

53. Ferber and Lynd, *The Resistance*, 201-21.

54. Jerry Elmer, Unpublished Paper (Providence, Rhode Island American Friends Service Committee, 1980); Ferber and Lynd, *The Resistance*, 201-21; *Peacemaker*, May 20, 1971 and July 7, 1973.

55. See the case of the "Camden 28," *New York Times*, May 20, 1972; also see *U.S. v. Baranski*, 484 F.2d 566 (7th Cir. 1973); *U.S. v. Turchick*, 451 F.2d 333 (8th Cir. 1971).

56. *Peacemaker*, May 20, 1972.

57. Ibid., February 26, 1972.

58. Ibid., February 26, 1972.

59. Ibid., May 26, 1973.

60. Ibid., November 18, 1972.
61. Ibid., October 9, 1971.
62. Ibid., February 22, 1969.
63. *Liberation*, May 1972.
64. *Peacemaker*, February 9, 1974; January 29, 1966; November 10, 1973; December 9, 1972; September 29, 1973; January 26, 1973.
65. *Peacemaker*, December 9, 1972; July 17, 1972; August 12, 1972; September 12, 1972.
66. *WRL News*, July-August, 1974.
67. Ferber and Lynd, *The Resistance*, 151-52.
68. *Human Events*, March 20, 1971, reprinted in *Congressional Record*, March 25, 1971, 8077.
69. *WRL News*, November-December 1970; Ferber and Lynd, *The Resistance*, 291-93.
70. *Human Events*, March 20, 1971.
71. Ibid.
72. *New York Magazine*, June 29, 1970, reprinted in *Congressional Record*, June 29, 1970, 21938. Also see, for example, the draft guide published by the Union for National Draft Opposition (UNDO). This manual described scores of tactics to confuse, frustrate, and stifle the Selective Service System through both overt and covert methods. The manual's stated goal was to put Selective Service "under a kind of citizen's arrest." UNDO, *I Say No*.
73. *Human Events*, March 20, 1971.
74. Ibid.
75. *U.S. v. Freeman*, 388 F.2d 246, 249 (1967).
76. See, for example, James White, "Processing Conscientious Objector Claims: A Constitutional Inquiry," 56 *Calif. Law Review* 652 (1968).
77. Ibid., 654.
78. *Cox v. U.S.*, 332 U.S. 442, 453 (1948).
79. See generally *Witmer v. U.S.*, 348 U.S. 375 (1955); *U.S. v. Mitchell*, 246 F.Supp. 874 (1965); *U.S. v. Garrity*, 433 F.2d 649, (8th Cir. 1970); *Petrie v. U.S.*, 407 F.2d 267, 272 (1969); Frederick Brown and Stephen Kohn, "Human Rights and Freedom of Conscience in Administrative Law," 61 *University of Detroit Journal of Urban Law*, Winter 1984.
80. Biskir and Strauss, *Reconciliation*, citing extrapolations from *Federal Offenders in United States District Courts*, 132.
81. *Peacemaker*, November 21, 1964.
82. *U.S. v. Mitchell*, 246 F.Supp. 874, 898 (D. Conn. 1965).
83. Ibid., 899, 907.

84. *Mitchell v. U.S.*, 386 U.S. 972 (1967).
85. *Peacemaker*, December 17, 1966.
86. Ibid.
87. Ibid., September 16, 1972.
88. Biskir and Strauss, *Reconciliation*, 132.
89. Ibid., 132.
90. Ibid., 130.
91. *New York Times*, May 20, 1972; June 20, 1972.
92. Ibid., May 21, 1973.
93. Ibid.
94. Ibid.
95. Ibid., May 22, 1973.
96. Ibid., May 21, 1973.
97. Statistics compiled by the author from the following sources: Bureau of Prisons, *Annual Report*, 1949–1977; Selective Service System, *Annual Report*, 1949–1976; U.S. Bureau of Census, *Historical Statistics of the United States*, 1975; Selective Service System, *Special Monograph No. 11: Conscientious Objectors*.
98. Biskir and Strauss, *Reconciliation*, 130.
99. Ibid., 115.
100. Statistics compiled by the author from sources cited in Note 97, above.
101. The last induction during the Vietnam War was on December 29, 1972. U.S. House of Representatives, Committee on the Judiciary, Subcommittee on Courts, Civil Liberties and the Administration of Justice, *Amnesty Hearings*, 157.
102. Ibid., 616.
103. Ibid., 597.
104. Presidential Proclamation No. 4483, January 21, 1977.

7

The Reemergence of
Registration Resistance

The resumption of contemporary draft prosecutions can be traced back to 1980. Shortly after the Soviet Union's military incursion into Afghanistan, President Jimmy Carter announced plans to reinstate draft registration. His speech was similar in its intent to Truman's 1948 State of the Union speech announcing the commencement of the Cold War draft. As had Truman, Carter recognized tacitly that a draft was not needed to repulse invasion. Carter called for the reinstatement of draft registration to "demonstrate [America's] "resolve as a nation."[1] But the mood of America in 1980 was not the Cold War mood that had permeated the country in 1948. During the first five years of draft registration, the law faced greater opposition than any draft law in American history.

Provisions in the Selective Service Act granted the President power to issue an executive proclamation requiring youth to register. But congressional approval was needed to allocate the $8.6 million needed by the Selective Service to run the program.[2] The usefulness, necessity, and merit of Carter's program were debated strenuously in Congress. Senator Mark Hatfield led an unsuccessful seven-day filibuster against the measure.[3] But on June 12, 1980, the Senate approved the bill by a 58–34 vote; later, the House approved it 234-168. Seven days later registration became law.[4] The 1980 registration law required young men to register for the draft at local post offices at the age of eighteen. Neither classification procedures nor actual inductions were called for, but the penalty for re-

fusing to register remained unchanged from the Vietnam era—
a maximum five-year prison sentence and a $10,000 fine.[5]

Opposition to this draft law was widespread. Within days of
Carter's State of the Union address, an already existing anti-
draft movement mushroomed. More than 350 local anti-draft
groups formed on campuses and in communities in every state
of the union. A national coalition of peace, religious, student,
and women's groups organized the national Coalition Against
Registration and the Draft (CARD).[6] According to a survey by
the War Resisters League, just three weeks after Carter's
speech, over 40,000 people participated in hastily organized
rallies across the United States.[7] In New York City, more than
2,000 gathered; at the University of California Berkeley cam-
pus, 2,500 assembled.[8] On March 22, 1980, a coalition of anti-
draft groups including CARD, the War Resisters League, the
National Student Association, and Ralph Nader's Public Research Interest Group held a rally of more than 30,000 people
in Washington, D.C., and a West Coast rally of 5,000 in San
Francisco.[9] These rallies were followed by a number of small
sit-ins at congressional offices and federal buildings, including
the local Senate offices of Senators Edmund Muskie of Maine,
Ted Kennedy of Massachusetts, and Lawton Chiles of Florida.[10]

Post offices were also a target. During the first two weeks
of registration, thousands of small demonstrations or pickets
were set up at post offices around the country. Picketers urged
young men either not to register or to seek draft counseling
prior to registration. According to accounts in *Resistance News*,
demonstrations "varied in size from one protester in Bartles-
ville, Oklahoma, to several thousand on a mass picket line in
New York City." Civil disobedience and arrests occurred in
many cities, including New York, Boston, San Francisco, Dav-
enport, Austin, Kansas City, Columbus, Chicago, and Hartford.[11]

Resistance to registration was so widespread that government policymakers expressed concern that the anti-draft
movement could grow into an effective anti-war movement. A
transcript of a private meeting of President Reagan's Military
Manpower Task Force, which included Selective Service Di-

rector Thomas K. Turnage, Secretary of Defense Caspar W. Weinberger, presidential advisor Edwin Meese III, and Assistant Secretary of the Navy for Manpower John S. Herrington, revealed considerable concern that the anti-draft movement would unite with the anti-nuclear movement.[12] These Reagan administration leaders wished to avoid a potential political storm caused by "highly visible" trials of draft resisters. Assistant Secretary of the Navy Herrington stressed this point when he said:

I think we ought to proceed really cautiously on this particular point. It would be a real rally point. I am not in principle against felony prosecution for this. . . . I think the cases should be quiet; and pick the right jurisdiction so you don't end up in New York or Chicago, and end up in Omaha or somewhere like that.[13]

Defense Secretary Weinberger agreed with Herrington and warned against a draft trial in Washington, D.C.

The final report of the Military Manpower Task Force expressed concern about the "social costs" of the registration program and warned that "divisiveness may result from enforcement of rules opposed by an active minority."[14]

COMPLIANCE

The proponents of draft registration have praised its accomplishments. Thomas K. Turnage, director of the Selective Service System, testified before Congress that registration was "clearly a success story."[15] Likewise, Herbert C. Puscheck, of the U.S. Army Readiness and Development Command Headquarters, carefully analyzed the compliance data and concluded that the "current program works, works well [and] is improving."[16] Both Turnage and Puscheck based their optimistic conclusions on the high number of registrants. Although almost 500,000 failed to register, close to 12 million youths had fulfilled the requirements of the law.[17]

But registration has been plagued with problems. First, although the overwhelming majority of youths has registered for the draft, the number of illegal nonregistrants has reached historic proportions. Nearly twice as many youths refused to register for the draft between 1980 and 1984 (estimated at 500,000)[18] than refused to register during the 1964–1973 Vietnam War period (estimated at 250,000).[19]

Second, the Government Accounting Office has estimated that 4 million registrants have failed to inform the Selective Service of their changed addresses.[20] Failure to notify the service of a change of address is a crime.[21] It also renders registration nearly useless, for it deprives the government of ready access to a section of the draft-age population in the event of a national emergency.

Third, registration itself does not measure the willingness of a young man to be drafted. Historically, most civil disobedience has occurred during induction, not registration. In the past, the overwhelming majority of COs registered for the draft. Resistance occurred after the local draft board ordered COs into the armed services.[22]

Fourth, extensive efforts to increase registration have not succeeded. Both the Selective Service System and the Department of Justice have initiated aggressive campaigns to bolster the registration program. They have indicted seventeen nonregistrants (as of Feburary 1985) and have mailed warning letters to thousands of youths whose names were obtained from Social Security, the Internal Revenue Service, state drivers' licenses, and commercially purchased lists. They have also deprived nonregistrants of all federal student financial aid and job assistance programs.[23] But noncompliance remains at record levels.

The prosecutorial problems facing the Department of Justice dwarf the compliance problems facing the Selective Service System. Assistant Attorney General D. Lowell Jensen admitted in a letter, obtained through the Freedom of Information Act, that the chances of prosecuting a "silent" or nonpublic nonregistrant were "probably the same as the chances he will be struck by lightning."[24] (A "silent" nonregistrant is someone who does not register for the draft, but does not inform the government or the press of his act of civil disobedience.)

Public nonregistrants present the Department of Justice with an entirely different set of problems. Assistant Attorney Gen-

eral Jensen recognized that "religious and moral" objectors
would be very "sympathetic defendants." He felt that such cases
would have the "least appeal" to U.S. Attorneys, who might
find it difficult to imprison a religious or moral conscientious
objector.[25] Jensen predicted that some public nonregistrants
would raise "selective prosecution" defenses.[26] The selective
prosecution defense is based on challenging the legality of an
indictment on First Amendment grounds. Public nonregistrants claim that they are being "picked out" and prosecuted
because they attack the draft openly, while silent nonregistrants, who do not engage in protected First Amendment
speech, escape prosecution.[27]

Selective Service and the Department of Justice have also
had considerable problems over the misidentification of nonregistrants. In one instance, Selective Service forwarded names
of suspected nonregistrants to the Justice Department. A subsequent FBI search identified one of the persons on the list as
an eighty-year-old retired minister who had sent a protest letter to Selective Service. When the error was discovered, Justice complained to Selective Service over the "waste of valuable FBI resources." Justice bluntly informed Selective Service that they had "other, perhaps more compelling matters"
to investigate and prosecute.[28]

An aggressive policy of prosecuting resisters would create an
entirely different set of problems for the government. The federal prison system does not have the capacity to handle a large
influx of draft resisters. In March 1984, the director of the
Federal Bureau of Prisons reported that the federal prison
system was "28% overfilled."[29] In any case, even if the government prosecuted a thousand resisters annually, it would require more than 500 years to deal with the 1980–1984 nonregistrants alone. Clearly, the incarceration of large numbers
of convicted draft resisters is presently impracticable.

Given the plethora of prosecutorial complications, fewer draft
prosecutions have occurred under the 1980 registration law
than under any other draft law in American history. In the
first five years of registration, only eighteen indictments were
handed down. As of June 10, 1985, ten defendants had been
convicted, and of those, convicted the average prison sentence

served has been approximately 42 days. Five indictments were dismissed.[30] Thus, the overwhelming majority of the 500,000 nonregistrants have escaped prosecution. Given the limitations on prosecutorial resources and prison space, the vast majority of nonregistrants never will be prosecuted.

The problems currently facing the registration program are enormous. If youth were again subjected to acutal induction into the armed services, the number of illegal resisters would no doubt increase dramatically. As in the Vietnam era, civil disobedience to the Selective Service Act remains a potent obstacle to the efficient administration of the draft.

THE DRAFT AND MILITARY POLICY

The anti-draft movement is based on a radical critique of current American military and foreign policy, and stands in sharp contrast to the political outlook of both major parties.[31] Congressional debate on the reintroduction of registration was indicative of the narrow military positions advocated on the Hill. Congressional supporters and opponents of legislation on the draft endorsed similar basic military premises. These premises, which underlie U.S. military and foreign policy, were identified in a bipartisan congressional report entitled *Military Policy and the All-Volunteer Force*:[32]

- "Any military action anywhere in the world other than a comparatively minor show of force would almost certainly require the augmentation of active duty forces with reserves and/or draftees."
- The present armed forces of 2.1 million on active duty and 877,000 in reserve are "at best an absolute minimum [force to] meet initial U.S. national security commitments worldwide."
- Manpower needs are determined by calculating U.S. need based on a "major war with the Soviet Union and its Warsaw pact allies."
- "The United States needs large conventional forces to permit responses to threats without resorting to strategic nuclear war."[33]

These assumptions were the starting point of the congressional debate.

Senator Mark Hatfield, for example, a prominent leader of congressional opposition to the draft, did not attack these basic assumptions. Instead, he argued that the army was presently viable, that the all-volunteer force was able to reach 99.1 percent of its recruitment goals; that "the quality of recruits [was] generally better than at any time in recent history"; and that registration would not significantly improve mobilization in times of a national emergency.[34] The supporters of registration agreed with similar military assumptions, but came up with different conclusions. Senator Harry Byrd, Jr., supported registration because it would "reduce substantially the time delay which would now occur between mobilization and induction."[35] Representative Richard White thought registration would add to the "power and strength" that was needed to preserve the peace.[36]

The draft resisters, in contrast, supported an entirely different vision of foreign and military policy, one in which military might was no longer the means by which America pursued its interests in the world. Instead, they urged that the underlying world problems—hunger, ignorance, exploitation—be addressed and resolved directly. Russell F. Ford, a public nonregistrant, wrote a letter to President Reagan, stating: "I say 'enough'! I refuse to kill. I will not cooperate with you in your murderous business from which some profit while others die."[37] Ford was indicted and found guilty of refusing to register for the draft.

Nonregistrant Christopher Clarke expressed his fears and concerns in a public letter:

The prospect of being imprisoned for five years frightens me. For the past four years my life has been continually put "on hold" as I have been reluctant to make plans which may come to nothing if interrupted by a sudden indictment. But to me my anguish seems trivial next to that of other people the government is asking me to terrorize in Grenada, in Lebanon, in Nicaragua and El Salvador, or any other place the U.S. Government feels it must impose its demands by means of brute military force. Five years is a small price to pay indeed to insure that one less American will stooge for a murderous foreign policy.[38]

A new and idealistic program for U.S. international relations was urged by nonregistrant Matt Nicodemus in his letter to President Reagan:

There is a world that I want us all to be able to live in. It is a world where all people live freely, openly and honestly. . . . It is a world where all people have enough food to eat, lead decent, healthy lives. It is a world where people resolve their disagreements through nonviolent means.[39]

CONCLUSION

On July 28, 1982, David Landau, of the Washington office of the American Civil Liberties Union, testified before a House subcommittee on the Selective Service Act. Landau told the congressmen: "We are witnessing one of the most massive demonstrations of civil disobedience in our Nation's history."[40] The 1980 anti-registration movement was a continuation of a nonviolent tradition initiated in 1658 when colonial settlers refused to fight and slaughter Indians. The ideas of Garrison, the tactics of the World War I and World War II resisters, and the revolutionary adjustments the movement made during the Cold War and Vietnam, all have contributed to making the contemporary movement potentially the most effective anti-draft movement in American history.

NOTES

1. *Congressional Digest*, April 1980.
2. *Congressional Quarterly Almanac*, 39, 41-46.
3. Ibid., 46.
4. Ibid., 46.
5. Title 50 U.S.C. 453, Jimmy Carter, Executive Proclamation 4471, July 2, 1980. Congress recently increased the penalty for draft resistance. As of December 31, 1984, the maximum fine was raised from $10,000 to $250,000 (see the Criminal Fine and Enforcement Act, 18 U.S.C. 3623). Prison sentences, starting November 1, 1986, will be increased from five to six years (see the Comprehensive Crime Control Act).
6. U.S. House of Representatives, Committee on the Judiciary,

Subcommittee on Courts, Civil Liberties, and the Administration of Justice, *Implications of Draft Registration*, 104.

7. Ibid., 33.

8. *New York Times*, February 13, 1980.

9. U.S. House of Representatives, *Implications*, 33. *Resistance News*, October 3, 1980.

10. *Resistance News*, October 3, 1980.

11. Ibid.

12. U.S. House of Representatives, *Implications*, and *Selective Service Act Prosecutions Hearings* (1982), 78-93. Also see *Washington Post*, May 19, 1982; *New York Times*, May 20, 1982.

13. *New York Times*, May 20, 1982.

14. Military Manpower Task Force, *A Report to the President on Selective Service Registration*, December 15, 1981.

15. Thomas K. Turnage, *Testimony Before the Subcommittee on HUD-Independent Agencies of the House Appropriations Committee*, February 23, 1983.

16. Herbert Puscheck, "Selective Service Registration: Success or Failure?" *Armed Forces and Society*, 23.

17. *Semiannual Report of the Director of Selective Service*, 2.

18. The exact number of nonregistrants is nearly impossible to determine. The General Accounting Office has estimated it to be as high as 700,000; the Selective Service System has estimated it to be 382,000. I have used a mid-range estimate of 500,000. See *Selective Service Semi-annual Report*, 2 and General Accounting Office, *Alternatives to Current Draft Registration Program Needed Unless Level of Compliance Improves*.

19. Lawrence M. Biskir and William A. Strauss, *Chance and Circumstance: The Draft, the War and the Vietnam Generation*, 86-87.

20. *Resistance News*, March 1984.

21. 50 U.S.C., 462.

22. Biskir and Strauss, *Chance and Circumstance*, 86-87.

23. Puscheck, "Selective Service Registration," 15, 18-20; *Selective Service Semiannual Report*, 5.

24. D. Lowell Jensen, Assistant Attorney General, Criminal Division, DOJ, to Herbert Puscheck, Associate Director of Selective Service, March 2, 1982 (FOIA, Kohn File).

25. D. Lowell Jensen to the Attorney General, Memorandum, July 26, 1982; and D. Lowell Jensen to Lawrence Lippe, Chief General Litigation and Legal Advice Section, Criminal Division, Department of Justice, March 23, 1982 (FOIA, Kohn File).

26. Ibid.

27. *U.S. v. Schmucker*, U.S. Court of Appeals for the 6th Cir., No. 82-3701 (November 25, 1983), but see *U.S. v. Wayte*, 710 F.2d 1385 (9th Cir. 1983). In a March 19, 1985, decision the Supreme Court upheld the constitutionality of the Department of Justice's "passive enforcement" program. This program limited prosecution to nonregistrants who either turned themselves in to the government, or who were identified by citizens as having failed to register. The Supreme Court did not foreclose First Amendment selective prosecution challenges. In order to make out a selective prosecution defense, the defendant must prove that the prosecution "had a discriminatory effect and that it was motivated by a discriminatory purpose." *Wayte v. U.S.*, 53 *Law Week* 4319, 4322 (March 19, 1985).

28. D. Lowell Jensen to Herbert C. Puscheck, Associate Director, Selective Service System, March 2, 1982 (FOIA, Kohn File).

29. Presently, the federal prisons hold only 31,262 inmates. They are 28 percent "overfilled" (*New York Times*, March 30, 1984).

30. Selective Service Semi-Annual Report, 1984, 11; Ann Clark, compilation for conscientious objectors, June 10, 1985 (Washington, D.C., 1985); National Resistance Committee, Status of Draft Registration Prosecutions (Boston: September 7, 1984); CCCO, Hotline No. 28 (Philadelphia, May 3, 1985); *The Reporter for Conscience's Sake*, January 1984; *Resistance News*, March 1984.

31. *Resistance News*, March 1984.

32. Robert Goldich, *Military Manpower Policy and the All-Volunteer Force*.

33. Ibid., 1, 2.

34. *Congressional Report*, April 1980.

35. Ibid., 108.

36. Ibid., 126.

37. *Peacemaker*, January 1982.

38. Letter of Christopher Clarke to U.S. Attorney Salvatore Martoche, reprinted in *Resistance News*, March 1984.

39. *Peacemaker*, February 1982.

40. House of Representatives, *Prosecutions*, 31.

8

The Evolution of Draft Law

The Selective Service Act is a repressive law. It criminalizes a wide variety of conduct, including counseling people to avoid the draft, destroying or burning draft cards, refusing to register for the draft, failing to possess a draft card, failing to report a change of address, failing to report for a military physical examination, and failing to report for induction into the armed services.[1] But over a period of thirty years, the courts have expanded the rights of registrants, conscientious objectors, and anti-draft activists. These legal reforms have enhanced the ability of youth to protest the draft and to receive legal exemption from conscription.

Conscription laws have survived a variety of broad constitutional attacks, including attempts to have them nullified as a violation of the First and Thirteenth Amendments. The courts also have rebuffed attempts to ban the use of the draft for illegal or undeclared wars of aggression.[2] Recently, the Supreme Court has rejected broad constitutional attacks on draft laws because they discriminate against women, penalize nonregistrants' college financial aid packages, and select for prosecution only vocal opponents of the draft.[3]

The constitutionality of the military draft was upheld unanimously by the Supreme Court during World War I. In *Arver v. U.S.* (1918)[4] the court held that Congress and the President had broad powers to establish draft boards and to conscript people under Article I, Section B of the U.S. Constitution. This section grants Congress the power to declare war and to raise and support armies. The court summarily dismissed First

Amendment arguments against conscription, ridiculing them as "unsound." The Thirteenth Amendment argument, that the draft constitutes involuntary servitude, was rejected as "refuted by mere statement." The Supreme Court abdicated any responsibility toward ensuring due process for conscientious objectors other than the statutory protection provided in the law.[5]

Just before the outbreak of World War II, Congress passed the Selective Service Act of 1940. This act incorporated a number of statutory liberalizations to the 1917 law. Induction would be run by local civilian draft boards, and conscientious exemptions would be determined by the draft board and not the military.[6] In addition, the grounds for exemption were broadened. In World War I, only certain and recognized pacifist churches were statutorily exempt. In World War II, specific church membership was no longer required; instead, pacifism could be based on strongly held "religious beliefs."[7]

The courts strictly interpreted the statutory language of the Selective Service Act, which entrusted the administration of the law, including the granting of conscientious objection exemptions, to the Selective Service System. Conscientious status was to be granted only by draft boards and not by the courts. In its 1945 opinion, *Estep v. U.S.* (1944), the Supreme Court made this point very clear, stating, "the courts are not to weigh the evidence to determine whether the classification made by the local board was justified. The decisions of the local boards made in conformity with the regulations are final, even though they are erroneous."[8]

Although the trial courts could not challenge factual determinations reached by the local draft boards, they could attack the process by which the local board reached its decision. The Supreme Court established this due process right in *Gibson v. U.S.* (1944).[9] In *Gibson* the court held that a registrant "may in defense to a criminal prosecution attack a board's order as arbitrary or illegal." Thus, by the end of World War II, decisions by a local draft board had to be made in "conformity with the regulations" and could not be "arbitrary or illegal."

When Congress passed the Selective Service Act of 1948, most of the statutory language from the World War II measure was incorporated into the body of the Cold War draft law. The Supreme Court and the local federal courts continued to develop a body of law protecting registrants' due process rights. In *Simmons v. U.S.* (1955),[10] the Supreme Court held that a registrant had the right to know what evidence his draft or appeals boards used in reaching their determinations. The court stated that "a fair resume [of the evidence] is one which will permit the registrant to defend against the adverse evidence—to explain it, to rebut it, or otherwise detract from its damaging force."

During the 1960s and 1970s, the lower courts followed the lead of the Supreme Court and expanded a number of due process rights. The U.S. Circuit Courts of Appeals held that draft boards could not take a registrant's "demeanor" into account when reaching a classification determination;[11] that failure to consider all the facts before the board was a denial of due process;[12] that failure to inform a registrant of new evidence against him was a violation of due process;[13] and that a registrant had the right to submit his case in writing to an appeals board.[14]

These court decisions prodded the Selective Service System to liberalize its regulations. In 1972 twelve "major" changes in the administration of the draft law were initiated.[15] Among the more significant changes were:

New Registration	Prior Regulation
Registrant was entitled to bring up to three witnesses to the personal appearance.	Registrant did not have right to bring witnesses to his personal appearance before a local board.
Personal appearance now allowed.	No personal appearance allowed at appeals board.
Reasons for adverse classification must be given to all registrants by both the local and the appeals boards.	Local board was not required to provide registrant with the reasons why his request was denied.

By the end of the Vietnam War, Selective Service law had become very sophisticated. Although a registrant's rights before a board were still limited, the growing body of procedural rights created a check against local board abuse and increased a young man's ability to be exempted legally from the draft.[16] These due process liberalizations worked hand-in-hand with a liberalization of the conscientious objector exemption.

Under the Selective Service Act, only those opposed to all wars on the basis of "religious training and belief" can obtain conscientious objector status. Although the law specifically states "religious," in two important Supreme Court cases the right to objector status was enlarged to include atheists and agnostics. Despite the statute's language, conscientious objection principles could be based on nonreligious grounds. In the landmark case of *U.S. v. Seeger* (1965),[17] the Supreme Court held that a registrant was no longer required to base exemption on belief in a God or a "Supreme Being." Instead, a "sincere or meaningful belief" which occupies a place "parallel to that filled by God" was enough to qualify for objector status. In *Welsh v. U.S.* (1970),[18] the court reaffirmed *Seeger* and explicitly included strongly held atheistic "moral" or "ethical" beliefs as adequate to meet the test for objector status.[19]

SELECTIVE PROSECUTION

Draft resisters were subject to extralegal government prosecution and surveillance throughout the Cold War and Vietnam War periods. In 1965, U.S. Attorney General Nicholas deB. Katzenbach announced the start of a "national investigation" to discover communists within the anti-draft movement.[20] Throughout the Vietnam period anti-draft movement activists were wiretapped, bugged, subjected to COINTELPRO operations, and infiltrated by *agents provocateur* working for the FBI and army intelligence.[21] But even before 1965, anti-draft activists faced repressive tactics from both the Department of Justice and the Selective Service System.

Selective Service and the Justice Department used two methods for suppressing critics of the draft: delinquency inductions and selective prosecution. These methods were developed during the late 1940s and were used extensively throughout the Cold War and Vietnam War periods, until the courts limited their use. Delinquency inductions occurred when the Selective Service picked out vocal opponents of the draft and ordered them to report immediately for active military duty. This process effectively removed dissidents from their local communities or universities. The "delinquents" were forced either to enter the military or go to jail.[22] In cases where a vocal opponent of the draft had received a draft deferment, such as conscientious objector or ministerial status, the deferment would be rescinded. Selective Service would reclassify the protesters as I-A and subject them to accelerated induction.[23]

The Department of Justice initiated a similar policy. Instead of prosecuting all potential evaders of the draft, the Justice Department aggressively went after only the most "willful instances" of draft refusal.[24] Such "selective prosecutions" singled out the most vocal opponents of the Selective Service Act for indictment. In Feburary 1950, the Central Committee on Conscientious Objectors (CCCO) criticized the political implications of this policy. CCCO pointed out that anti-draft activists would be targeted by the Justice Department for prosecution.[25]

The Selective Service System justified these measures, pointing to the dangerous foreign policy implications of "unrealistic" draft protesters. The director of Selective Service wrote: "It is an even smaller group now which, mistaken in its evaluation of international relations, refuses to recognize reality and claims in the name of liberty and privilege, destructive of national unity, that circumstances are different."[26]

From 1948 until 1967, selective prosecution and delinquency induction were actively pursued as policies by the Selective Service System and the Justice Department. As protests to Vietnam grew in size and popularity, opposition to these discriminatory policies grew. There was a strong public outcry in 1966, when eleven students who sat-in at the Ann Arbor draft board lost their student deferments.[27] Public reaction "so intensified by late fall that the Justice Department and Selective Service issued a joint declaration suggesting that the punitive policy would be dropped.[28] But within a year Selective Service reaffirmed a modified delinquency induction policy. "Legal" protesters would not suffer, but:

when ordinarily peaceful and orderly demonstrations and dissentions [sic] degenerate into activities which hamper, impede, or obstruct the System's or related military manpower procurement processes, this constitutes a failure of the registrant to meet the conduct required to retain a deferment and in addition may become the basis for a determination of delinquency.[29]

Selective Service Director Lewis B. Hershey also pointed to the "upsurge" in public protests to the "increased draft calls" as a justification for continued selective induction.[30]

Although the precise number of delinquency inductions is difficult to determine, Robert Goldstein, in his study of political repression in the United States, states that "between December 1, 1967 and December 1, 1968, 537 students who turned in their draft cards lost their student deferments and were declared eligible for induction."[31]

The Supreme Court struck down delinquency inductions in *Oestereich v. Selective Service Board* (1968).[32] In this case the court held that Selective Service could not reclassify an otherwise exempt person in retaliation for anti-war protests. James J. Oestereich, a divinity student exempted from the draft, mailed in his draft registration card as a protest against the Vietnam War. In retaliation, his local board took away his deferment. The Supreme Court voided this reclassification: "Once a person registers and qualifies for a statutory exemption, we find no legislative authority to deprive him of that exemption because of conduct or activities unrelated to the merits of granting or continuing that exemption."[33]

Two years later, in *Gutknecht v. U.S.* (1970),[34] the Supreme Court voided the accelerated induction of protesters. David Earl Gutknecht had returned his registration certificate to the government to protest the war. In retaliation, his local board accelerated his induction date, assigning him "first priority in the order of induction," and placing his name ahead of many other nonprotesting potential inductees. The court struck down this practice, stating that Congress intended illegal protest activity to be punished through the criminal process, not internal Selective Service processes. The court stated that the Selective Service System was not a "free-wheeling agency meting out their own brand of justice in a vindictive manner."[35]

The Justice Department also practiced selective prosecution of vocal draft resisters. But it appears clear that some forms of selective prosecution are illegal. Toward the end of the Vietnam War, the U.S. Seventh Circuit Court of Appeals struck down the practice as unconstitutional.

In *U.S. v. Falk* (1975), Jeffrey Falk, an active member of CADRE (Chicago Area Draft Resisters) was indicted under the Selective Service Act. A federal district judge found Falk guilty. Falk appealed his conviction on grounds of illegal selective prosecution. The Court of Appeals found that there was substantial evidence to support Falk's contention that he was selected for prosecution in retaliation for exercising his constitutionally protected right of free speech:

In the present case there are several indications this was exactly the purpose of the prosecution. At the close of the trial Falk's attorney asked the assistant U.S. Attorney who tried the case be called as a witness, and offered to prove that the Assistant U.S. Attorney had told Falk's attorney . . . that he knew of defendant's draft counseling activities, that a good deal of trouble in enforcing the draft laws came from people such as Falk . . . that defendant's draft-counseling activity was one of the reaons why prosecution for non-possession of draft card was brought.[36]

The court held that this example of selective prosecution of draft law violators was illegal.

In *Wayte v. U.S.* (1985),[37] the Supreme Court upheld the constitutionality of the government's contemporary "passive enforcement" policy. Under this policy, the Justice Department limited prosecutions of nonregistrants to those who either reported themselves to the government or who were turned in by other citizens. David Wayte, a nonregistrant, wrote several letters to the Selective Service System and the President, stating that he had not registered for the draft. For example, in a letter to Selective Service, he wrote, "I have not registered for the draft. I plan never to register. I realize the possible consequences of my action, and I accept them."[38] The Department of Justice indicted Wayte under the passive enforcement program. Wayte challenged the indictment as a violation of his First Amendment rights. But the Supreme Court rejected this claim and upheld the indictment.

The court did not reject selective prosecution as a potential defense in a draft case. Indeed, the court recognized the applicability of the selective prosecution defense if the indicted nonregistrant could demonstrate that the prosecution "had a discriminatory effect and was motivated by a discriminatory motive."[39] The court held that Wayte could not meet this burden:

He has not shown that the enforcement policy selected nonregistrants for prosecution on the basis of their speech. . . . The Government did not prosecute those who reported themselves but later registered. Nor did it prosecute those who protested registration but did not report themselves or were not reported by others. In fact, according to the Supreme Court the Government did not even investigate those who wrote letters to Selective Service criticizing registration unless their letters stated affirmatively that they had refused to comply with the law.[40]

The *Wayte* holding could facilitate the prosecution of vocal nonregistrants active in the anti-war movement. But it was not a repudiation of the *Falk*, *Oestereich*, and *Gutknecht* line of cases. Selective prosecution, under the right circumstances, remains a valid defense in a draft law case.

CONCLUSION

Both the expansion of a registrant's due process rights before the draft board and the liberalization of the conscientious objector exemption have broadened the ability of people to obtain legal exemption from the draft. Likewise, the successful attacks on selective inductions and prosecutions have protected the rights of anti-draft political activists. But regardless of these liberalizations, the law remains repressive. The Selective Service Act makes a broad variety of anti-war activities illegal and creates hardships for sincere conscientious objectors.

NOTES

1. See Title 50 U.S.C. 462; *Gara v. U.S.*, 340 U.S. 857 (1950); *U.S. v. O'Brien*, 391 U.S. 367 (1969); *U.S. v. Houseman*, 338 F.Supp. 854 (1972); *U.S. v. Demangone*, 456 F.2d 807 (1972); *U.S. v. Heywood*, 469 F.2d 602 (1972); *Lowe v. U.S.*, 389 F.2d 51 (1968); *Cahoon v. U.S.*, 152 F.2d 752 (1946).

2. *Arver v. U.S.*, 245 U.S. 366 (1918); *U.S. v. O'Brien*, 391 U.S. 367 (1968); *Mitchell v. U.S.*, 386 U.S. 972 (1967).

3. *Rostker v. Goldberg*, 453 U.S. 57 (1981)—male-only draft registration does not violate the equal protection clause; *Selective Service System v. Minnesota Public Int. Research*, 453 U.S. 57 (1984)—the Solomon Act amendments, which deny federal financial assistance to nonregistrants, are not unconstitutional; *Wayte v. U.S.*, 53 U.S. *Law Week* 4319 (March 19, 1985)—the Department of Justice's "passive enforcement" policy is not unconstitutional selective prosecution.

4. 245 U.S. 366 (1918).

5. See discussion of *Arver* in Harry Peck, "Selective Service: Right to Counsel, Due Process, and the First Amendment," 51 *Marquette L. Rev.* 407 (Wis. 1968), 421.

6. Selective Service System, *Monograph No. 11*, 69.

7. Ibid., 68.

8. 327 U.S. 144 (1944).

9. 67 S.Ct. 301 (1946).

10. 348 U.S. 397 (1955).

11. 476 F.2d 254 (1973).

12. 473 F.2d 1225 (1973).

13. 442 F.2d 383 (1971).

14. 415 F.2d 389 (1970).

15. Selective Service System, *Monograph No. 11*, 2.

16. James White, "Processing Conscientious Objector Claims: A Constitutional Inquiry," 56 *Calif. L.R.* 652 (1968).

17. 380 U.S. 163 (1965).

18. 398 U.S. 333 (1970).

19. For a discussion of whether a person has a constitutional right to be exempted from military service on the grounds of conscience, see Justice William O. Douglas' dissent in *Gillette*; *U.S. v. Macintosh*, 283 U.S. 605, 624 (1931); *Girouard v. U.S.*, 328 U.S. 61, 68-9 (1946). Also see Frederick Brown, Stephen Kohn, and Michael Kohn, "Conscientious Objection: A Constitutional Right," unpublished paper (1985).

20. *New York Times*, October 18, 1965.
21. Robert J. Goldstein, *Political Repression in Modern America: 1820 to the Present*, 443, 450, 458.
22. Bureau of Census, 1143.
23. Selective Service System, *Annual Report for 1966*, 43.
24. *NewsNotes*, February 1950.
25. Ibid.
26. Selective Service System, *Annual Report*, 1966.
27. Michael Useem, *Conscription, Protest, and Social Change*, 102.
28. Ibid., 103.
29. Ibid.
30. Selective Service System, *Legal Aspects of SS-47*.
31. Goldstein, *Repression*, 439.
32. 393 U.S. 233 (1968).
33. Ibid., 237.
34. 396 U.S. 295 (1970).
35. Ibid., 304.
36. 479 F.2d 616 (1973).
37. *Wayte v. U.S.*, 53 *Law Week* 4319 (March 19, 1985), 37.
38. Ibid., 4320.
39. Ibid., 4322.
40. Ibid.

9

The Draft and Social Change

The anti-draft movement raises important questions regarding the legal system, political power, and methods of achieving peace and social change in the United States. The movement has operated outside of the political party structure; it has never run a candidate or received the support of any major political party. Since the War of 1812, every bill establishing a national draft that has been introduced by a President has been approved by Congress.

Resisting the draft, or urging others to resist the draft, is illegal. This simple reality has forced the movement to operate outside of the basic "democratic" structure of the American political system. Pacifist resisters have always been in the minority. Yet despite their unpopularity and numerical weakness, resisters have had a substantial impact on American public policy. This phenomenon has defied the predictions of both Establishment and radical critics.

CRITICS LOOK AT THE ANTI-DRAFT MOVEMENT

Radical critics of the anti-draft movement argued that a social change program based on personal resistance would be ineffective or counterproductive during the Vietnam War. They ridiculed resistance, calling it an ineffective method of ending the war. Fred Halstead, a socialist and a leader of many of the largest anti-Vietnam War demonstrations, presented a "Marxist" critique of the draft resistance in his comprehensive study of the Vietnam War protests, *Out Now*. Halstead presented five major criticisms of the draft protesters:

1. Draft resisters were isolated in American society, and "revolutionaries should not purposely isolate themselves from the working class youth."[1]

2. The draft was a secondary issue to the broader issue of opposing the Vietnam War: "[The anti-draft movement] tries to organize the sentiments of scared students who want to stay out of the army rather than build a movement directed squarely against the Johnson administration."[2]

3. Spending time in jail was a waste—it could be better spent organizing against the war.

4. Because the vast majority of the American people were not pacifists and were not "opposed on principle to all military service" as were many of the resisters, draft protests were not an effective way to reach the American people and were not a correct way to approach the reality of American politics.

5. Anti-war activists who entered the armed forces could potentially build an effective protest movement from within the military.[3]

Many of the largest anti-war organizations adopted Halstead's analysis and rejected the promotion of draft resistance. In 1967, for example, a meeting of the Student Mobilization Committee refused to adopt a resolution calling for the "promotion" of draft resistance. Instead, it passed a resolution that supported "the right of individuals to refuse to cooperate with the military system."[4] Halstead's analysis was based on a very pragmatic view of draft resistance. The correct Marxist position on the draft, he said, should reject the "philosophical or spiritual imperatives" of the resistance, and realistically accept the fact that only a tiny percentage of people would ever resort to its tactics. He claimed that it was thus doomed to fail.[5]

The major deficiencies of Halstead's analysis were, first, his underestimation of the power of nonviolent resistance; second, his failure to take into consideration historical examples of successful civil disobedience campaigns; and third, his failure to anticipate the growth and impact of the anti-draft movement on the Selective Service System.

Nonviolent civil disobedience is a qualitatively different form of protest activity or tactic than either electoral politics or legal demonstrations. Although civil disobedience has never been the most popular or widespread protest method in the United States, its history is extensive and at times it has been quite successful. Halstead completely ignored the historical examples in which small groups of dedicated activists violating unjust laws achieved significant victories. Among the examples that must be taken into account are the resistance of Quakers to oppressive religious laws in the colonies; the resistance of the Founding Fathers to the Stamp Act and Tea Tax; the abolitionist resistance to the fugitive slave laws; the jailing of suffragists prior to the passage of the Twentieth Amendment; the "free speech fights" of the labor movement; and the sit-ins of the modern civil rights movement.[6]

Most historians of nonviolent civil disobedience have recognized the influence of this tactic on American politics. For example, David Weber, in *Civil Disobedience in America*, states that "the potential for civil disobedience lies deep in the mainstream of American attitudes and thought . . . advocates of civil disobedience in our history have been numerous, influential, and extraordinarily varied . . . it has been a felt presence in American thought and life out of all proportion to its number."[7]

Not only does nonviolent civil disobedience have a long tradition in the United States, but also America itself was the birthplace of some of the basic theories of nonviolent resistance. According to Leo Tolstoy, one of the greatest pacifists in world history, William Lloyd Garrison, was the first person to outline the political doctrine of nonviolent resistance to oppression. Nonviolent direct action was not a doctrine developed by Tolstoy in Russia or by Mohandas Gandhi in India. Although each of these thinkers influenced the development of the theory, its origin can be traced to a politicization of the religious tactics of the Quakers first formulated by Garrison and the members of the New England Non-Resistance Society. Staughton Lynd, in *Nonviolence in America*, points out this historical development:

It is often supposed that nonviolence is a philosophy conceived by Gandhi and Tolstoy and recently imported into the United States by Martin Luther King, Jr. The fact is that a distinctive American tradition of nonviolence runs back to the seventeenth century. Thoreau's influence on Gandhi is well-known. Tolstoy, too, was indebted to American predecessors. In "A Message to the American People," written in 1901, Tolstoy stated that "Garrison, Parker, Emerson, Ballou, and Thoreau . . . specifically influenced me." Three years later Tolstoy wrote that "Garrison was the first to proclaim this principle [of nonresistance to evil] as a rule for the organization of man's life."[8]

Although Halstead was correct in identifying the numerical weakness of the draft resistance movement, he failed to understand that the strategy of civil disobedience can succeed without the large numbers of participants that an electoral strategy requires. The history of civil disobedience has shown the power of dedicated minorities who have refused to cooperate. Henry David Thoreau, in his famous essay "Civil Disobedience," clearly recognized this political fact: "A minority is powerless while it conforms to the majority; it is not even a minority then; but it is irresistible when it clogs by its whole weight."[9] Halstead also ignored the substantial impact the resistance movement had on the ability of Selective Service to induct young men into the armed forces, and the importance of the movement in hastening the abolition of the Cold War draft in 1973.[10]

Michael Useem, in *Conscription, Protest, and Social Change*, offers a different critique of the anti-draft movement. Useem, who supported the tactic, states that the Vietnam resistance movement failed. According to Useem, the anti-draft movement reached a climax in 1969 and then collapsed and died. He offers a number of reasons in support of this position:

1. The end of the social conditions responsible for the rise of resistance, and the appearance after 1969 of other, more legitimate channels for draft or war protest. Because "new

means for effective political expression became available," people had less reason or need to resort to civil disobedience."[11]

2. Internal conflicts within the anti-draft organizations: "Frequently identified problems include excessive militancy, inflexible leadership . . . unstable coalitions, oligarchic tendencies, sectarian quarrels, and weak internal coordination."[12]

3. The failure to reach and organize working-class, poor, and black youth. Useem claims that the absolutist resistance tactic alienated many working-class youth from the movement.[13]

4. The failure to achieve "massive proportions": "In its failure to reach the necessary level of strength, the Resistance served as an outright refutation of the theory behind preemptive resistance." Quoting from a former resistance activist, Useem continues, "[resistance] hasn't worked, so you have to assume the original idea was just not feasible . . . it really didn't stop the draft system, and draft resistance doesn't deal with anything really political."[14]

Although Useem identifies a number of valid weaknessess of the Vietnam-era movement, his major contentions that the anti-draft movement declined after 1969 and that it failed to have impact are completely wrong. There was no decline in the anti-draft movement after 1969; in fact, the movement reached its apex in 1972–1973. Between 1963 and 1973 both the number of conscientious objectors and the number of indictments for Selective Service Act violations increased continuously.[15] Even as the number of inductees into the armed forces declined, the number of protesters rose. For example, in 1969 there were 1,744 indictments under the draft law. In 1972 the number rose to 4,906. At the same time the total number of inductions fell dramatically from 262,646 in 1969 to a mere 25,273 in 1972.[16] In the same year, more conscientious objector exemptions were granted than people were inducted into the military. Also in 1972, almost 20 percent of inductees violated the draft law and were indicted.[17]

Although a number of anti-draft organizations folded after

1969, the draft resistance movement continued to grow both in numbers and in political impact. The decline of anti-draft organizations and the increase of resisters is not contradictory. The vast majority of anti-war conscientious objectors have never been active in major anti-draft organizations. Regardless of the war, resisters have come from a broad range of religious and political backgrounds and have been members of many different organizations and societies, or members of no organization. Draft resistance is a profoundly individual act. For some it is a moral choice, for others a political or religious imperative—but regardless of where a resister grounds his conviction, the actual choice is subjective. The organizational requirements of a resistance movement are very different from mainstream or even radical political movements. Resisters are drawn from a wide variety of religious, political, and moral subcultures and societies. Useem is wrong to look at the problems within a small group of resistance organizations and conclude that the movement had died.

Useem's theory that "legitimate" channels for anti-war organizing opened up after 1968 and that this contributed to the decline of draft resistance is also incorrect. Although the McCarthy and McGovern presidential campaigns opened up some channels for young activists, the resistance movement continued to grow throughout the 1960s and 1970s. In fact, as opposition to the war increased, more and more people joined the draft resistance movement and refused to cooperate with Selective Service. Useem also overlooks the fact that draft resistance cannot be channeled as can other protest movements. When an individual is confronted with an induction notice, the choice is simply whether to cooperate or to resist. It is hard to coopt a person who faces prison for his beliefs. An electoral campaign or a massive public demonstration cannot negate the moral and personal choice resisters face when confronted by the draft notice or induction into the aimed services. Thus, civil disobedience has often been used as a tactic when electoral or legal procedures cannot immediately resolve the problem at hand: If a runaway slave pounds at one's door asking for help, does one violate the Fugitive Slave Act and render assistance, or does one follow the law and turn the slave over to the authorities?

Another group of theorists argues that the anti-draft movement was an important arm of the anti-war movement. Michael Ferber and Staughton Lynd, in *The Resistance*, conclude that the anti-draft movement not only helped force the United States out of Vietnam but also altered the course of American foreign policy: "Thus a strong case can be made that draft resistance set limits on the escalation of the Vietnam War. Even more clearly it limited the government's capacity to wage future wars by critically delegitimizing conscription in the eyes of America's youth."[18]

Ferber and Lynd cite a number of articles and sources to portray the serious "domestic costs" to the Johnson and Nixon administrations created by the resistance movement: "McGeorge Bundy, one of the chief architects of the Kennedy-Johnson policy in Southeast Asia . . . said he now believed the domestic costs of the war to be 'plainly unacceptable.' He cited 'the growing bitterness and polarization of our people,' and then added: 'There is a special pain in the growing alienation of a generation which is the best we have had.' "[19]

Although Ferber and Lynd's analysis of the anti-draft movement is largely correct, their expectations of its potential may have been excessive. They thought it would grow into a massive anti-state movement and present a powerful challenge to the American government. They saw in the growing draft resistance movement a tributary of a broader movement for radical reform:

America's young people have begun to question the existence and location of power itself. . . . [And] there remains a growing trend toward liberation from all repressive centers of authority, personal and political, left, right, and corporate.[20]

Lynd and Ferber cite the Quaker social philosopher Kenneth Boulding to support this analysis: " 'The draft may well be regarded as a symbol of a slow decline in the legitimacy of the national state.' "[21]

The abolition or destruction of the American government was not the primary goal of most draft resisters. Delegitimization of the government was an indirect byproduct of drafting soldiers to fight in a senseless war. Draft resisters were primarily sincere pacifists or people who detested the Vietnam War. The Vietnam-era draft resistance did not lead to the massive delegitimization predicted by Ferber and Lynd. The government did not ignore the growing delegitimization caused by the resistance movement; instead, it yielded to the resistance. The courts liberalized their procedures and reduced sentences;[22] draft calls decreased and eventually the draft was abolished.

Although Ferber and Lynd's expectation of a mass anti-state movement did not materialize, their overall analysis of the anti-draft movement is extremely insightful. They were not misled by the initial smallness and unpopularity of the draft resistance, and they managed to look beyond certain statistical facts and weaknesses in the movement to gain a better understanding of its true political and social meaning.

DRAFT RESISTANCE AND AMERICAN DEMOCRATIC THEORY

The anti-draft movement raises serious questions about the nature of the American political system. The resistance was primarily an illegal movement existing outside of the traditional electoral avenues of influence on public policy. Both the "consensus" and "pluralist" interpretations of American politics fail to explain fully the political theory behind the resistance movement. To understand the proper role of draft resistance within the American system, one must take a new look at the very foundations of American democracy. Civil disobedience is not an anomaly within the republican system of government. Indeed, disobedience is both legitimate and a necessary check on state oppression.

According to the consensus theory, the United States' political tradition is one of substantial unity of opinion on all the basic questions concerning the body politic. For example, Thomas Dye and L. Harman Zeigler, in the *Irony of Democracy*, state: "The success of the economic system has helped to smother class differences, which in any case have never been as strong in America as in most other Western democracies. . . . The explanation for the broad popular consensus in America rests ultimately in the fact that capitalism as an economic system has been extremely successful."[23] The consensus viewed was repeated by historian Richard Hofstadter:

> The fierceness of the political struggles has often been misleading; for the range of vision embraced by the primary contestants in the major parties has always been bounded by the horizons of property and enterprise . . . the business of politics—so the creed runs—is to protect this competitive world . . . above and beyond temporary and local conflicts there has been a common ground, a unity of cultural and political tradition, upon which American civilization has stood. The culture has been intensely nationalistic and for the most part isolationist.[24]

The anti-draft movement cannot be explained by the consensus model. The movement has, for the most part, been illegal and outside of the mainstream of the political system. Its major actors have been political prisoners—outcasts and convicts—not lawyers and professionals. If the American "consensus" is widened to include these dissident activists, the utility of the theory is greatly diminished. The organized anti-draft movement also strikes at the very foundation of the notion of consensus. Peace, not economic advantage, rests at the foundation of the movement's foreign policy goals. Third World liberation, not the containment of communism, is the premise of its international outlook. The anti-draft movement attacks both conscription and the standing army. Unilateral disarmament is placed on the agenda. The movement rejects the tactic of compromise and negotiation which structures so much of the mainstream political life—replacing the "deal" with moral conviction. The tactics and goals of the anti-draft movement do not neatly conform to the consensus view of American politics, and this view fails to provide an analytical model for interpreting the resistance movement.

The pluralist model also fails to explain fully the growth of and effectiveness of the anti-draft movement. Robert Dahl, in

A Preface to Democratic Theory, summarizes the political theory of pluralism as follows:

A central guiding thread of American constitutional development has
been the evolution of a political system in which all the active and
legitimate groups in the population can make themselves heard at
crucial stages in the process of decision . . . decisions are made by
endless bargaining; perhaps in no other national political system in
the world is bargaining so basic a component of the political process.[25]

Draft resistance is not based on a conception of politics that
begins with the "bargaining" process. The fundamental act of
draft resistance is the withdrawal of cooperation and support
from an immoral or bad system. It is the Garrisonian command of complete passive resistance to evil, or Thoreau's idea
of a resister becoming a "clog" that interferes with the ability
of the system to operate. The emphasis of resistance is on direct action, rather than on voting, or setting up special interest groups, or seeking input into the government. Freedom does
not come from the vote or from constitutions, according to resistance philosophy, but from direct action. William Lloyd
Garrison and his supporters refused to participate in the electoral process. Similarly, the anti-draft movement never has
taken on a major electoral expression. Thoreau explained the
difference between voting and direct action in his essay on civil
disobedience: "Even voting *for the right* is *doing* nothing for
it. It is only expressing to men feebly your desire that it should
prevail. A wise man will not leave the right to the mercy of
chance."[26]

Thoreau explained that the philosophical premise behind civil
disobedience is a distrust of the majority to do what is right.
History demonstrated to Thoreau that governments rarely accept radical ideas for change. With poetic candidness, Thoreau asked:

Why is it [government] not more apt to anticipate and provide for
reform? Why does it not cherish its wise minority? Why does it cry
and resist before it is hurt? Why does it not encourage its citizens to
be on the alert to point out its faults, and do better than it would

have them? Why does it always crucify Christ, and excommunicate Copernicus and Luther, and pronounce Washington and Franklin as rebels![27]

For those in the war resistance movement, legal dissent along the pluralist model is not enough. To cooperate is to allow the terror to exist. Draft resisters have always been a minority. Their ability to effect change would be meaningless without the civil disobedience tactic. Nonviolent civil disobedience breaks from the limitations of electoral democracy and representative government and entrusts power directly to the people. This power can be abused, but it is also a power that—in the words of Roger Nash Baldwin—has proven "socially useful."[28] Civil disobedience gave anti-war principles a reality with which the government was eventually forced to come to terms.

How should civil disobedience be squared with American political theory? What is the proper role of illegal action within a democratic form of government? Opponents of civil disobedience commonly respond to these questions by raising the specter of anarchy. If everyone broke laws they did not like, so the argument goes, the government and social fabric would collapse.[29] In fact, under the U.S. Constitution, civil disobedience is both legitimate and proper.

Exploration of the roots of the legality of nonviolent direct action and civil disobedience requires a second look at the very nature of the constitutional system. The common understanding of the American political system sees the basic power allocation of the national government as two-fold. First, power is divided between the states and the national government. Certain powers are reserved only to the states, while others are under federal jurisdiction.[30] Second, the national government itself is divided into three branches—the executive, legislative, and judicial—each with its own power and responsibility.[31]

If our understanding of the government remains confined to this scheme, civil disobedience will be illegal once the legislature has passed a bill, the executive has signed it into law, and the courts have upheld its constitutionality. Within this scheme, political power rests with either elected or appointed elites. Logically, political effectiveness would be understood in the context of the powers wielded by the elites and the methods to influence the thinking of the elites. But this simple picture of the U.S. government is fundamentally flawed and historically incorrect. The basis of the government of the United States was *not* a compromise between the states and the national government. Instead, it was a three-part compromise between the states, the national government, and "the People." Civil disobedience is a right vested within the jurisdiction of the People.

The Wisconsin Supreme Court recognized the tripartite nature of the federal system in a historic decision that found the Fugitive Slave Act of 1850 unconstitutional. (This decision was overturned on the merits by the U.S. Supreme Court in *Ableman v. Booth*.)[32] Although the holding of the Wisconsin court would not survive the pro-slavery U.S. Supreme Court, it clearly encompassed the tripartite compromise of the federal Constitution: "The constitution of the United States is, in its more essential and fundamental character, a *tripartite* instrument. The parties to it are: THE STATES, THE PEOPLE and THE UNITED STATES. The latter is, indeed, a resulting party, brought into existence by it."[33]

Abolitionists challenged the Fugitive Slave Law of 1850 and the institution of slavery itself as unconstitutional because it violated natural rights protected under the Constitution. These natural rights were retained by the People, and no government had the legitimate power to negate them. Charles Olcott, an abolitionist attorney, made this point in an 1838 article: "Governments and laws are established, not to *give*, but to protect . . . rights. [They are] made to protect the *whole* of the rights of their subjects; not to annul or diminish them. Their great . . . end . . . is to preserve men's rights."[34]

The Founding Fathers of the United States recognized this tripartite agreement. After the U.S. Constitution was written, the Constitutional Convention authorized a letter by General George Washington to the state governments transmitting the new constitution and requesting approval by the states. In this letter, Washington clearly recognized the sovereign sphere of the People within the new government:

Individuals entering into society, must give up a share of liberty to
preserve the rest. The magnitude of the sacrifice must depend as well
on situation and circumstance, as on the object to the [sic] obtained.
It is at all times difficult to draw with precision a line between those
rights which must be surrendered, and those which may be reserved.[35]

Thus, at the essence of America's governmental structure the
People maintain certain rights and give up other rights. But
the People, as a separate entity whose sphere is recognized by
the government, exists and in it are vested certain natural and
positive rights.

When Representative James Madison of Virginia proposed
the Bill of Rights in the First Congress of the United States,
he proposed it in part to calm the fears of many Americans
that the new central government would encroach on the powers reserved to the People. Madison wrote:

I believe that a great mass of the people who opposed it [the Consti-
tution], disliked it because it did not contain effectual provisions
against the encroachments on particular rights, and those safe-
guards which they have been long accustomed to have interposed between them and the magistrate who exercises the sovereign power;
nor ought we consider them safe, while a great number of our fellow-
citizens think these securities necessary.[36]

The Bill of Rights was proposed to set forth some of the specific rights retained by the People, rights with which the government could not interfere, such as freedom of religion, speech,
press, assembly, and the right to trial by jury. The Tenth
Amendment of the U.S. Constitution explicitly reserved to the
states and the "People" rights and privileges that were not
mentioned in the Constitution.[37]

Within the American framework of government, not only are
the People a separate and legitimate arm of the government,
but they are also potentially the most powerful force. The people created the government, and they retain the duty and power
to destroy the government. English common law tradition recognized this power of the People to resist or abolish government. During the trial of Thomas Baird for sedition in En-

gland (1817), the discussion during the trial made the historic traditions of resistance quite clear.

> The doctrine of resistance belongs to the more sacred and private recesses of the constitution, which are profaned by exposure to the eyes and to the handling of the vulgar. Yet our safety undoubtedly might come to rest on the principle of resistance . . . clearly the doctrine of resistance is recognized among all who have studied our constitution, and how boldly it is held forth, even by the official advisers of the crown, as the ultimate resource which the constitution affords when an extreme case shall arrive.[38]

According to the philosophy of resistance, as understood in England prior to the American Revolution, people maintained the right to alter or abolish unjust governments. This philosophy was adopted by the Founding Fathers and underlies the entire spirit of the American system. To repeat the inspiring words of the American Declaration of Independence:

> We hold these truths to be self-evident: that all men are created equal; that they are endowed, by their Creator, with certain inalienable rights; that among these are life, liberty, and the pursuit of happiness. That to secure these rights, governments are instituted among men, deriving their just powers from the consent of the governed; that whenever any form of government becomes destructive to these ends, it is the right of the people to alter or abolish it, and to institute a new government, laying its foundation on such principles.[39]

At the very foundation of our system is the fundamental right of people to question and challenge the powers of the government. These rights can be lawfully executed by agitating along the lines explicitly protected under the Bill of Rights. But they are not limited by the Bill of Rights. Direct action and civil disobedience are constitutionally recognized by the very spirit and underlying premises of the U.S. government.

Thus, the spirit of the American system recognizes two fundamental principles: first, that there exists a third branch of federal power—the People—and second, that the People have a right to resist government and the laws. The right to resist not only is a theoretical right, but is also codified in the Constitution by the provisions protecting the right to trial by jury. The trial by jury was one of the few methods developed to protect people from the "oppression of government." Sir William Blackstone, in his famous commentaries on the English common law, stated that the jury was a "barrier" between the "liberties of the people" and the "prerogative of the crown." It allowed the executive power to be placed with the "prince," yet any criminal judgment would need the "unanimous suffrage of twelve of his [the defendant's] equals and neighbors."[40]

Many of the Founding Fathers spoke highly of the jury power, including John Adams, Alexander Hamilton and the famous colonial attorney Andrew Hamilton. During the debates concerning the ratification of the U.S. Constitution in the Massachusetts convention, one delegate pointed to the jury power as the primary check against improper "usurpation" by the new federal government:

The people themselves have in their power effectually to resist usurpation, without being driven to an appeal to arms. An act of usurpation is not obligatory; it is not law; and any man may be justified in his resistance. Let him be considered as a criminal by the general government, yet only his fellow-citizens can convict him; they are his jury, and if they pronounce him innocent, not all the powers of Congress can hurt him; and innocent they certainly will pronounce him.[41]

The U.S. Supreme Court has recognized consistently that the "purpose of the jury trial . . . is to prevent oppression by the government."[42] The court has also taken note of the importance that jury power played within the Founding Fathers' understanding of American democracy: "On many occasions, fully known to the Founders of this country, jurors—plain people—have manfully stood up in defense of liberty against the importunities of judges and despite prevailing hysteria and prejudices. The acquittal of William Penn is an illustrious example."[43]

Essential to the operation of the laws of the United States is the existence of a small group of lay-people with unreviewable power to find a criminal defendant innocent of a crime. Congress can pass a criminal statute, and the courts can find it constitutional. The executive can spend millions of dollars on its enforcement, but only a jury comprised of lay-people can convict. The jury power was one of the powers the U.S. Constitution did not take away from the jurisdiction of the People. The jury has the constitutional and nonreviewable right to acquit a defendant in a criminal trial. Regardless of the law violated or the amount of evidence against the accused, regardless of the witnesses or confessions, and regardless of a frank confession of guilt to the crime charged, the jury retains the ultimate power to acquit.

Not only were juries given the final power to convict or acquit a criminal defendant, but they were also vested with the power to ignore the law and acquit a defendant despite the fact that the defendant broke the law.[44] The famous legal thinker and former dean of the Harvard University School of Law, Roscoe Pound, spoke of this power:

Jury lawlessness is the greatest corrective of law in its actual administration. The will of the state at large imposed on a reluctant community, the will of a majority imposed on a vigorous and determined minority, find the same obstacle in the local jury that formerly confronted kings and ministers.[45]

Thus, juries have the power to acquit war resisters or other activists who engage in civil disobedience. Juries have the power to legalize resistance. A person who engages in civil disobedience cannot be found guilty unless representatives of the People so decide. But the jury power has been severely limited by modern court decisions.

When the Republic was founded, juries were regularly informed of their power to acquit a criminal defendant even if the defendant had violated the law. Jurors were instructed to judge both the *law* and the fact in cases they heard. But during the nineteenth century there was a shift away from this practice. Judges stopped informing jurors of their nullification powers. Today it is the common practice for judges to instruct jurors only to decide *facts*. The morality of the law was placed beyond the reach of the jury.[46] A U.S. Court of Appeals decision explained this shift in the powers of the jury:

The youthful passion for independence accommodated itself to the reality that the former rebels were now in control of their own destiny, that the practical needs of stability and sound growth outweighed the abstraction of centrifugal philosophy, and that the judges in the courts, were not the colonial appointees protecting royalist patronage and influence but were themselves part and parcel of the nation's intellectual mainstream.[47]

In most war resister cases, the defendant is denied the right to tell the jury why he broke the law. The issue of conscientious objection or the morality of a war is never presented to the jury. Instead, the jury hears only the most narrow issue: Did the defendant register for the draft? Did the defendant report for induction? (One of the few exceptions was the trial of the "Camden 28," in which the judge allowed the jury to hear evidence concerning both the morality of the Vietnam War and the defendants' justifications for their actions.)

The judge's right to refuse to inform the jury of its nullification powers in war resistance trials was upheld by the U.S. Federal Court of Appeals for the District of Columbia Circuit in *U.S. v. Dougherty*.[48] In that decision the court recognized the power of the jury to ignore the law. But the court upheld the trial judge's refusal of a defense request that the jury be informed of these constitutional powers. The majority opinion stated that allowing such an instruction might lead to "anarchy" and burden jurors with "overwhelming" moral responsibility that would create an "extreme burden for the jurors' psyche."

Justice David Bazelon strongly dissented. He felt that juries had a right to be informed of their constitutional powers:

The very essence of the jury's function *is* its role as spokesman for the community conscience *in* determining whether or not blame can be imposed. . . . If revulsion against the war in Southeast Asia has reached a point where a jury would be unwilling to convict a defendant for commission of the acts alleged here, we would be far better advised to ponder the implications of that result than to spend our time devising stratagems which let us pretend that the power of nullification does not even exist.[49]

Juries have the ultimate power to legalize civil disobedience. But this power has been limited seriously by the refusal of courts to allow jurors to be informed of their powers.

As the Founding Fathers of the United States rightly recognized, civil disobedience and resistance to unjust laws are an integral part of the American democratic tradition. Civil disobedience is one of the greatest checks against oppression and tyranny in the American system. Prior to the Revolution, the Founding Fathers engaged in civil disobedience against the British. After independence, radicals and reformers used civil disobedience to fight slavery; to gain rights for women, labor, and minorities; and to struggle for peace. Civil disobedience is a direct appeal to the conscience of the People. Its strategy is the refusal to cooperate with unjust laws. It is a direct challenge to policies condemned by resisters as being contrary to the laws of nature or the legitimate exercise of state power. Civil disobedience is a lawful conflict between the People and the Sovereign.

NOTES

1. Fred Halstead, *Out Now! A Participant's Account of the American Movement Against the Vietnam War*, 170.

2. Ibid., 170, citing a speech of Socialist Worker's Party leader Doug Jenness.

3. Ibid., 172.

4. Ibid., 296.

5. Ibid., 167.

6. See generally David Weber, *Civil Disobedience in America*; Staughton Lynd, *Nonviolence in America: A Documentary History*; Judith Stiehm, *Nonviolent Power*; Peter Brock, *Pacifism in the United States—from the Colonial Era to the First World War*; Mulford Q. Sibley, *The Political Theories of Modern Pacifism*.

7. Weber, *Civil Disobedience*, 11, 17, 18.

8. Lynd, *Nonviolence*, xv.

9. Ibid., 70.

10. See Chapter 6, 00-00, for statistics on the collapse of the draft.

11. Michael Useem, *Conscription, Protest, and Social Change*, 287.

12. Ibid., 265.

13. Ibid., 271.

14. Ibid., 276.

15. Statistics compiled by the author; Lawrence M. Biskir and William A. Strauss, *Reconciliation After Vietnam: A Program of Relief for Vietnam-Era Draft and Military Offenders*, 130.

16. Ibid.; Biskir and Strauss, *Reconciliation*, 130.

17. Ibid.; Biskir and Strauss, *Reconciliation*, 15.

18. Michael Ferber and Staughton Lynd, *The Resistance*, 287.

19. Ibid.

20. Ibid., 289.

21. Ibid., 388.

22. Statistics compiled by the author; Biskir and Strauss, *Reconciliation*, 130.

23. Dye and Zeigler, cited in Robert J. Goldstein, *Political Repression in Modern America: 1870 to the Present*, xi.

24. Richard Hofstadter, *The American Political Tradition*, xxvii, xxxix.

25. Robert Dahl, *A Preface to Democratic Theory*, 137, 150.

26. Henry David Thoreau, *On the Duty of Civil Disobedience*, reprinted in Lynd, *Nonviolence in America*, 64.

27. Ibid., 67.

28. Roger Nash Baldwin, interview with author, Summer 1981.

29. See, for example, majority opinion in *U.S. v. Dougherty*, 473 F.2d 1113 (1972).

30. U.S. Constitution.

31. Ibid.

32. *Ableman v. Booth*, 62 U.S. 509 (1858).

33. *In re Sherman Booth*, 3 Wis. 1 (1854).

34. Howard Jay Graham, "The Early Antislavery Backgrounds of the Fourteenth Amendment," *Wis. L.R.* (Wis. 1950), 626, 627.

35. Richard Perry and John Cooper, eds., *Sources of Our Liberties: Documentary Origins of Individual Liberty in the United States Constitution and the Bill of Rights*, 418g (hereinafter *Sources*).

36. Ibid., 421.

37. U.S. Constitution.

38. *Proceedings in the High Court of Justiciary at Edinburgh Against A. M'Laren and Thomas Baird for Sedition*, 57 George III 105, 107, (1817).

39. Perry and Cooper, *Sources*, 319.

40. (*Williams v. Florida*, 90 S.Ct. 1893, 1905 (1970).) Blackstone, cited in *Duncan v. Louisiana*, 88 S.Ct. 1444, 1448-49 (1968).

41. Massachusetts Delegate Theophilus Parsons, quoted in *Sparf and Hansen v. U.S.*, 156 U.S. 51, 144 (dissent by Justice Horance

Gray). Statements by John Adams appear at *Sparf and Hansen*, 143-44; statements by Alexander Hamilton appear at *Sparf and Hansen*, 147; and Andrew Hamilton's statement to the jury in the *John Peter Zenger Trial* appear at *Sparf and Hansen*, 146. The early American history concerning jury power is fully spelled out in Supreme Court Justice Horance Gray's dissent in *Sparf and Hansen*, 110-83.

42. *Williams v. Florida*; *Reid v. Covert*, 354 U.S. 1 (1956).

43. *U.S. v. Quarles*, 76 S.Ct. 1 (1955).

44. *1 Burr's Trial* 470 (1808); *Sparf v. U.S.*, 156 U.S. 51 (1895). The U.S. Supreme Court, in *Georgia v. Brailsford*, 3 Dall. 1, 4 (1794), explicated the court's early understanding of the jury power. The court was clear, a jury had the power and right to decide questions of both fact and law: " . . . it must be observed that by the same law which recognizes this reasonable distribution of jurisdiction, you have nevertheless a right to take upon yourselves to judge of both, and to determine the law as well as the fact in controversy."

45. Roscoe Pound, "Law in Books and Law in Action," 44 *Am. L. Rev.* 12, 18 (1910), cited in *U.S. v. Dougherty*, 473 F.2d 1113, 1132 (D.C. Cir. 1972).

46. B. Becker, "Jury Nullification," *Trial Magazine*, October 1980, 44.

47. *U.S. v. Dougherty*, 473 F.2d 1113 (D.C. Cir. 1972).

48. 473 F.2d 1113 (1972).

49. Ibid., 1144.

10

Conclusion: The Courage of Peace

In 1838, William Lloyd Garrison presented the "Declaration of Sentiments" to the Boston Peace Convention. He called for a new era of resistance to war. He warned that difficulties would face the new movement: "In entering upon the great work before us, we are not unmindful that in its prosecution we may be called to test our sincerity, even if in fiery ordeal. It may subject us to insult, outrage, suffering. Yet, we anticipate no small amount of misconception, misrepresentation, calumny."

Draft resisters have known "insult, outrage, suffering." The movement has been opposed actively by Congress, the courts, the executive branch, and mainstream public opinion. Almost 10,000 anti-war conscientious objectors have been imprisoned. A handful have died. Thousands have been permanently scarred from the effects of imprisonment and the stigma of a felony conviction. Yet over the years the movement has survived, grown, and blossomed into a force that seriously imperils the very existence of a draft in the United States.

When American wars appeared popular and necessary, the resisters' protests were mocked as fanatical and were suppressed as treasonous. When the first American troops engaged in combat in Vietnam, the political idealism of the young anti-draft activists appeared as impotent as their predecessors. But the Vietnam draft resisters were not operating in a historical vacuum. They inherited a tradition of theory and practice that enabled them to cope with prison and social isolation. Important laws were liberalized, and generations of imprisoned veterans from previous wars stood ready to help the new generation. The movement adjusted its ideology and tactics to the Cold War.

As the Vietnam War dragged on and lost the support of the American people, the anti-draft movement flourished. There were more conscientious objectors, more indictments, and more opposition to the draft than ever before in American history. By the early 1970s the draft had collapsed. More than 200,000 nonregistrants remain undetected, thousands of young men were under indictment and ready for prison, and a mass, public movement against conscription had been created. The courts were growing increasingly reluctant to imprison sincere objectors. Nonviolent direct action had succeeded in frustrating the Selective Service System and perhaps in altering U.S. military policy. An anti-draft movement finally succeeded. The new anti-registration movement, following in the footsteps of the Vietnam movement, may grow to pose an equally effective opposition to any new draft laws.

But has the sacrifice of thousands of war resisters been worth the modest results of the movement? Prison is never a desirable end. It has broken too many spirits and stolen too many years ever to be glamorized. Yet thousands went to jail instead of to the battle front. During the Vietnam War billions of dollars were spent to wage a useless war against the people of Indochina. Millions died, including more than 59,000 Americans. Hundreds of thousands of others suffered permanent disabilities. Is it possible to compare sacrifices? No. But it is imperative that society fully recognize and appreciate the sacrifice, courage, and legitimacy of conscientious objection and resistance to war.

The *type* of questions draft resisters raised stands in sharp contrast to the official debates on the draft, which center almost entirely on military manpower options. Lacking in these debates are the moral questions concerning war, peace, foreign policy, and the viability of nonviolence in world affairs. No one questions whether the military should exist. No one raises the issue of whether killing is right or wrong—rather, the question is how to kill, with nuclear bombs or with conventional troops. No one asks whether war is a legitimate tool for the implementation of foreign policy. The questions revolve around when to go to war, for what reasons, and against which enemy. The anti-draft movement, however, raises fundamental questions in an uncompromising manner. It questions the morality of an assumed reality.

Warfare has fundamentally changed. The advent of nuclear war has given added power and appeal to the nonviolent philosophy of draft resistance. The inhuman barbarism of nuclear holocaust has forced new generations to reevaluate their willingness to support warfare in any capacity. The courage and heroism associated with the glories of former wars have faded. Where is the young boy who dreams of growing up to lead the battle of Hiroshima? These radical changes in the nature of warfare have forever altered the role of the military in modern society. Parades, medals, and reminders of battlefield exploits are becoming aspects of antiquity. The Nuclear Veteran, the Agent Orange Veteran, and the Vietnam Veteran are slowly replacing the Veterans of Iwo Jima and D-Day.

Draft resisters have pioneered a new form of courage—the courage of peace.

Bibliography

The available literature on draft resistance is far from comprehensive. The few published books have focused on resistance during a specific war and have not attempted to tie together the entire history of the movement. Prior to the publication of *Jailed for Peace*, a complete study of draft resistance has yet to appear.

Because of the limited secondary sources, I have carefully reviewed the primary source collections that contain information on the anti-draft movement. A number of these collections are a gold mine of unexplored data on draft resistance, and include letters from conscientious objectors, diaries, transcripts of court statements, confidential military and government memoranda on resisters, and other historical material. Newspaper accounts and the *Congressional Record* were also very valuable resources.

I interviewed former imprisoned conscientious objectors, government officials, anti-war activists, and contemporary nonregistrants. Among those interviewed were former Attorney General Ramsey Clark, the founder of the American Civil Liberties Union and imprisoned World War I objector Roger Nash Baldwin, War Resisters League staff member and imprisoned World War II resister Ralph DiGia, author and Cold War resister Gene Sharp, and Jerry Elmer, a staff member of the Rhode Island American Friends Service Committee convicted of destroying draft records during the Vietnam War. Files from the Selective Service System and the Criminal Division of the Department of Justice were obtained through use of the Freedom of Information Act.

IMPORTANT SPECIAL COLLECTIONS

Princeton University, American Civil Liberties Union (ACLU). This collection contains exhaustive and invaluable records regarding draft resistance during World War I, including unpublished diaries, letters from imprisoned objectors, accounts of prison conditions throughout the United States, newspaper clipping files, and internal ACLU memoranda.

National Archives and Record Service, Military Intelligence Division Record Group (NA). Although most of the files of the Federal Bureau of Investigation and other government intelligence services are classified or otherwise unavailable for public inspection, all of the investigative files of the Department of War's Military Intelligence Division (MID) from 1917 to 1941 have been placed on public file at the National Archives. These records contain extensive holdings of anti-war pamphlets and materials, and provide a unique look into government attitudes and investigatory procedures with regard to the World War I and early World War II resisters.

Brandeis University, ACLU World War II files on microfilm (BU). The records of the ACLU national board on conscientious objectors have been placed on microfilm. I reviewed these records at Brandeis University. They contain extensive newspaper clippings on objector cases, case files on hundreds of objectors, and information on political conscientious objection.

Swarthmore University Peace Collection (SPC). The Peace Collection is the major national repository for American pacifist and anti-war literature and newspapers. Scores of resistance organizations have donated their files to the Peace Collection, including the War Resisters League and the American Friends Service Committee.

NEWSPAPERS AND MAGAZINES

The Absolutist (New York)
Armed Forces and Society (Washington, D.C.)
Boston Globe (Boston)
Call (New York)
Chicago Defender (Chicago)
Chicago Tribune (Chicago)
Civil War Times (Harrisburg, Penn.)
Congressional Digest (Washington, D.C.)
Congressional Quarterly Almanac (Washington, D.C.)
Congressional Record (Washington, D.C.)
The Conscientious Objector (New York)
Counterspy (Washington, D.C.)
El Imparcial (Puerto Rico)
Emancipation (Washington, D.C.)

Grapevine (New York)
The Guardian (New York)
International Socialist Review (Chicago)
Liberation (New York)
The Liberator (New York)
The Los Angeles Times (Los Angeles)
The New York Times (New York)
The New York World (New York)
PM Magazine (New York)
CCCO NewsNotes (Philadelphia)
The Peacemaker (Garberville, Calif.)
The Reporter for Conscience's Sake (Washington, D.C.)
Resistance News (California)
San Juan Star (San Juan, Puerto Rico)
The Selective Service System's newspaper clipping files (Washington, D.C.)
Survey (New York)
Vicksburg Sunday Post (Mississippi)
Washington Peace Center *Newsletter* (Washington, D.C.)
Washington Post (Washington, D.C.)
Wire City Weekly (Fort Leavenworth)
Win (New York)
WRL News (New York)

CASES

Ableman v. Booth, 62 U.S. 506 (1858)
Albany v. U.S., 152 F.2d 266 (1945)
Ruiz Alicia v. U.S., 180 F.2d 870 (1950)
Arver v. U.S., 245 U.S. 266 (1918)
Baldwin v. N.Y., 399 U.S. 66 (1970)
In re Sherman Booth, 3 Wis. 1 (1854)
Brown v. Louisiana, 447 U.S. 323 (1980)
1 Burr's Trial, 470 (U.S. 1808)
Cahoon v. U.S., 152 F.2d 752 (1946)
The Case of the Imprisonment of Edward Bushell for Alleged Misconduct as a Juryman, 6 State Trials 999, 22 Charles II (1670).
Clay v. U.S., 403 U.S. 698 (1971)
Cox v. U.S., 332 U.S. 442 (1948)
DuVernay v. U.S., 394 F.2d 979 (1968)
Estep v. U.S., 327 U.S. 114 (1946)
Everett v. U.S., 336 F.2d 979 (1964)

Ex Parte Green, 123 F.2d 862 (1941)

Galloway v. U.S., 319 U.S. 372 (1942)

Gara v. U.S., 340 U.S. 857 (1950)

Georgia v. Brailsford, 3 Dall. 1 (1794)

Gibson v. U.S., 329 U.S. 338 (1946)

Gillette v. U.S., 401 U.S. 437 (1971)

Girouard v. U.S., 328 U.S. 61 (1946)

Gutknecht v. U.S., 396 U.S. 295 (1970)

Hamilton v. Regents, 293 U.S. 245 (1934)

Hideichi Takeguma v. U.S., 156 F.2d 437 (1946)

Holmes v. U.S., 391 U.S. 936 (1968)

Joseph v. U.S., 405 U.S. 1006 (1972)

Kiyoshi Okamoto v. U.S., 152 F.2d 905 (1945)

Kneedle v. Lane, 45 Pa. 238 (1863)

Lowe v. U.S., 389 F.2d 51 (1968)

Lutfig v. McNamara, 373 F.2d 664 (1967)

Macintosh v. U.S., 42 F.2d 845 (1930)

Mitchell v. U.S., 386 U.S. 972 (1967)

Oestereich v. Selective Service Board, 393 U.S. 233 (1968)

Oestereich v. Selective Service System Local Board No. 11, 280 F.Supp. 78 (1968)

Petrie v. U.S., 407 F.2d 267 (1969)

Reid v. Covert, 354 U.S. 1 (1957)

Rostker v. Goldberg, 453 U.S. 57 (1981)

Selective Service System v. Minnesota PIRG, 453 U.S. 57 (1984)

Sellers v. Laird, 395 U.S. 950 (1969)

Shigeru Fujii v. U.S., 148 F.2d 298 (1945)

Simmons v. U.S., 348 U.S. 397 (1955)

Singer v. California, 380 U.S. 24 (1965)

Sparf and Hansen v. U.S., 156 U.S. 51 (1895)

Totus v. U.S., 39 F.Supp. 7 (1941)

The Trial of William Penn and William Meade at the Old Bailey, 6 State Trials 951, 22 Charles II (1670)

U.S. v. Baranski, 484 F.2d 556 (1973)

U.S. v. Demangone, 456 F.2d 807 (1974)

U.S. v. Dougherty, 473 F.2d 1113 (1972)

U.S. v. Downer, 140 F.2d 317 (1944)

U.S. v. Falk, 479 F.2d 616 (1973)

U.S. v. Feliciano-Grafals, 309 F.Supp. 1292 (1970)

U.S. v. Freeman, 388 F.2d 246 (1967)

U.S. v. Fujii, 55 F.Supp. 920 (1944)

U.S. v. Garrity, 433 F.2d 649 (1970)

U.S. v. Gutknecht, 283 F.Supp. 949 (1968)

U.S. v. Gutknecht, 406 F.2d (1969)

U.S. v. Henderson, 180 F.2d 711 (1950)

U.S. v. Heywood, 469 F.2d 602 (1972)

U.S. v. Houseman, 338 F.Supp. 854 (1972)

U.S. v. Kelly, 473 F.2d 109 (1971)

U.S. v. Lewis, 275 F.Supp. 1013 (1967)

U.S. v. Macintosh, 283 U.S. 605 (1931)

U.S. v. Miller, 131 F.Supp. 88 (1955), affirmed 233 F.2d 171 (1956)

U.S. v. Mitchell, 246 F.Supp. 874 (1965)

U.S. v. Mohammed, 288 F.2d 236 (1961)

U.S. v. Nelson, 476 F.2d 254 (1973)

U.S. v. Neptune, 337 F.Supp. 1028 (1972)

U.S. v. O'Brien, 391 U.S. 367 (1968)

U.S. v. Quarles, 350 U.S. 11 (1955)

U.S. v. Rauch, 491 F.2d 552 (1974)

U.S. v. Rehfield, 416 F.2d 273 (1969)

U.S. v. Rosebear, 500 F.2d 1102 (1974)

U.S. v. Schmucker, U.S. Court of Appeals for the 6th Circuit Slip
    Opinion, No. 82-3701 (November 25, 1983)

U.S. v. Seeger, 380 U.S. 163 (1965)

U.S. v. Smith, 249 F.Supp. 515 (1966)

U.S. v. Spock, 416 F.2d 165 (1969)

U.S. v. Turchick, 451 F.2d 333 (1971)

U.S. v. Valentine, 288 F.Supp. 957 (1968)

U.S. v. Vargas, 370 F.Supp. 908 (1974)

U.S. v. Wayte, 710 F.2d 1385 (1983)

Warren v. U.S., 177 F.2d 596 (1949)

Wayte v. U.S., 53 *Law Week* 4319 (March 19, 1985)

Welsh v. U.S., 398 U.S. 333 (1970)

Williams v. Florida, 90 S.Ct. 1893 (1970)

Williams v. U.S., 406 F.2d 704 (1969)

Witmer v. U.S., 348 U.S. 375 (1955)

SECONDARY SOURCES

American Civil Liberties Union. *Conscientious Objectors: The Facts
    Today*. ACLU Collection (hereinafter ACLU), 1920.

American Friends Service Committee. *The Draft, Its Impact on Poor
    and Third World Communities*. San Francisco: AFSC, n.d.

Arendt, Hannah. *Eichmann in Jerusalem: A Report on the Banality
    of Evil*. N.Y.: Viking Press, 1963.

Bach, John. *Danbury: Anatomy of a Prison Strike.* New York: WRL Reprint, 1972.

Baldwin, Roger Nash. *The Individual and the State.* ACLU, 1918.

Ballou, Abin. *Christian Non-Resistance in All Its Important Bearings.* Boston Public Library special collection, 1846.

———. *Evils of the Revolutionary War.* Brown University, John Hay Library special collection, 1846.

Barnet, Richard. *The Lean Years: Politics in the Age of Scarcity.* New York: Simon and Schuster, 1980.

Bartlett, John Russell, ed. *Records of the Colony of Rhode Island and Providence Plantations in New England.* New York: AMS Press, 1968.

Bennett, James. *Federal Prisons 1943.* A Review of the Work of the Federal Bureau of Prisons During the Year Ending June 30, 1943. El Reno, Oklahoma: Federal Prison Industries, Inc., 1944.

Berrigan, Daniel. *Absurd Convictions, Modest Hopes: Conversations After Prison with Lee Lockwood.* New York: Vintage Books, 1972.

Berrigan, Philip. *Of Beasts and Beastly Images: Essays Under the Bomb.* Portland, Oreg.: Sunburst Press, 1978.

———. *Writings from Jail: Within the Prison Gates.* New York: Touchstone Books, 1973.

Biskir, Lawrence M., and William A. Strauss. *Chance and Circumstance: The Draft, the War and the Vietnam Generation.* N.Y.: Knopf, 1978.

Biskir, Lawrence M., and William A. Strauss. *Reconciliation After Vietnam: A Program of Relief for Vietnam Era Draft and Military Offenders.* South Bend, Ind.: Notre Dame Press, 1976.

Black, Forrest. "The Selective Draft Cases, A Judicial Milepost on the Road to Absolutism." 11 *Boston U. L. R.* 37 (1931).

Boyle, Beth. *Words of Conscience: Religious Statements on Conscientious Objection.* Washington, D.C.: NISBCO, 1983.

Brock, Peter. *Pacifism in the United States—From the Colonial Era to the First World War.* Princeton: Princeton University Press, 1968.

———. *Radical Pacifist in Antebellum America.* Princeton: Princeton University Press, 1968.

———. *Twentieth Century Pacifism.* New York: Nostrand Reinhold, 1970.

Brown, Frederick, and Stephen Kohn. "Human Rights and Freedom of Conscience in Administrative Law." 61 *University of Detroit Journal of Urban Law* (1984) 177.

Brown, Frederick, Stephen Kohn, and Michael Kohn. "Conscientious Objection: A Constitutional Right." Unpublished paper, 1985. Author's file.

Browning, Frank, ed. *Prison Life: A Study of the Explosive Conditions in America's Prisons.* New York: Harper Colophon Books, 1972.

Burritt, Elihu. *Passive Resistance.* Reprinted in Staughton Lynd, ed., *Nonviolence in America: A Documentary History.* Boston: Bobbs-Merrill, 1966.

———. *A Plan of Brotherly Copartnership of the North and South.* New York: Dayton and Burdick, 1856.

Camus, Albert. *Neither Victims nor Executioners.* New York: War Resisters League reprint, n.d.

Chaffe, Zechariah, Jr. *Freedom of Speech.* New York: Harcourt Brace and Howe, 1920.

Channing, Edward. *A Century of Colonial History 1660–1760.* Vol. 3 of *A History of the United States.* New York: Macmillan Co., 1932–1937.

Chicago Area Draft Resisters (CADRE). *Behind Bars.* Chicago: Cadre, n.d.

Comfort, William. *William Penn and Our Liberties.* Philadelphia: Philadelphia Yearly Meeting, 1947.

Committee for Amnesty. *Still No Amnesty.* Swarthmore Peace Collection (hereinafter SPC), 1947.

Cornell, Julien. *Conscience and the State.* New York: Garland Publishers, 1973.

———. *The Conscientious Objector and the Law.* New York: John Day Co., 1943.

Cover, Robert. *Justice Accused: Antislavery and the Judicial Process.* New Haven: Yale University Press, 1975.

Crosby, Ernest. *Garrison, the Non-Resistant.* New York: J. S. Ozer, 1972.

Dahl, Robert. *A Preface to Democratic Theory.* Chicago: University of Chicago Press, 1956.

Dellinger, David. *Revolutionary Nonviolence.* Indianapolis: Bobbs-Merrill, 1970.

Delton, Carol, and Andrew Mazer. *Everyone's Guide to Non-Registration.* San Francisco: Regional Youth Adult Project of Northern California, 1980.

Eichel, Julius. *The Judge Said "20 Years."* New York, 1981.

Elliot, Jonathan. *The Debates in the Several State Conventions on the*

Adoption of the Federal Constitution. Philadelphia: J. B. Lippincott, 1896.

Elmer, Jerry. Unpublished paper. Providence: Rhode Island American Friends Service Committee, 1980.

Fay, Sidney. *The Origins of the World War*. Riverside, N.J.: Macmillan, 1959.

Fein, Helen. *Accounting for Genocide: National Responses to Jewish Victimization During the Holocaust*. New York: Free Press, 1979.

Fellowship of Reconciliation (FOR). *The Meaning of Korea*. SPC, 1950.

Ferber, Michael, and Staughton Lynd, *The Resistance*. Boston: Beacon Press, 1971.

Finney, Torin. "Practical Catholic; The Life and Times of Ben J. Salmon, 1889–1932." Masters Thesis, University of Massachusetts: Boston, 1984.

Fitzpatrick, John C., ed. *Journals of the Continental Congress 1774–1789*. Washington, D.C.: GPO, 1904–1937.

———. ed. *The Writings of George Washington*. Vol. 1, 1745–1756. Washington, D.C.: GPO, 1931.

Foner, Jack D. *Blacks and the Military in American History*. New York: Praeger, 1974.

Freeman, Harrop. *The Constitutionality of Peacetime Conscription*. Philadelphia: Pacifist Research Bureau, 1944.

Friedman, Leon. "Conscription and the Constitution: The Original Understanding." 67 *Mich. L.R.* 1493 (1969).

Friends Committee on National Legislation. *Resolutions Against Universal Military Training*. Washington, D.C.: AFSCNL, 1947.

Gandhi, Mohandas. *Nonviolence in Peace and War, 1942–1949*. New York: Garland Publishers, 1972.

———. *Nonviolent Resistance*. New York: Schocken Books, 1961.

Gara, Larry. *War Resistance in Historical Perspective*. New York: War Resisters League, n.d.

Garrison, William Lloyd. *The Abolition of Slavery, the Right of the Government Under the War Power*. Boston: R. F. Wallcut, 1861.

———. *Declaration of Sentiments*. Reprinted in Staughton Lynd, *Nonviolence in America: A Documentary History*. Indianapolis: Bobbs-Merrill, 1966.

Gaylin, Willard. *In the Service of Their Country: War Resisters in Prison*. New York: Grosset and Dunlap, 1970.

General Accounting Office (GAO). *Alternatives to Current Draft Registration Program Needed Unless Level of Compliance Improves*. Washington, D.C.: GAO, 1982.

Goldich, Robert. *Military Manpower Policy and the All-Volunteer Force.* Washington, D.C.: Congressional Research Service, 1981.

———. *Recruiting, Retention, and Quality in the All-Volunteer Force.* Washington, D.C.: Congressional Research Service, 1981.

Goldstein, Robert J. *Political Repression in Modern America: 1870 to the Present.* New York: Schenkman Publishing Co., 1978.

Graham, Howard Jay. "The Early Antislavery Backgrounds of the Fourteenth Amendment." *Wis. L. R.* (1950), 600.

Graham, John. *A Constitutional History of the Military Draft.* Minneapolis: Rossi and Hains, 1971.

Gray, Harold. *Character "Bad": The Story of a Conscientious Objector.* Kenneth Irving Brown, ed. (New York: Harper and Bros., 1934.

Gregg, Richard. *The Power of Nonviolence.* New York: Schocken Books, 1966.

Grosser, Philip. *Uncle Sam's Devil's Island.* SPC, 1933.

Halstead, Fred. *Out Now! A Participant's Account of the American Movement Against the Vietnam War.* New York: Monad Press, 1978.

Harris, David. *Goliath.* New York: Sidereal Press, 1970.

Hassler, Alfred. *Conscripts of Conscience.* SPC, 1942.

———. *Diary of a Self Made Convict.* Chicago: H. Regnery Co., 1954.

Hatfield, Mark O. "Draft Registration: Simple Prudence or a Dangerous Sign of Desperation." 17 *Willamette L.R.* 1 (1980).

Hazard, Samuel, ed. *Pennsylvania Colonial Records.* New York: AMS Press, 1976.

Headley, Joel T. *Pen and Pencil Sketches of the Great Riots.* New York: E. B. Trent, 1882.

Hershberger, Guy. *War, Peace and Nonresistance.* Scottdale, Penn.: Herald Press, 1944.

Hirst, Margaret E. *The Quakers in Peace and War.* London: Swarthmore Press, 1923.

Hofer, David. *Desecration of the Dead.* ACLU, n.d.

Hofstadter, Richard. *The American Political Tradition.* New York: Alfred A. Knopf, 1948.

Holley, Cantine, and D. Rainer. *Prison Etiquette.* Bearsville, N.Y.: Retort Press, 1950.

Hughan, Jessie. *Three Decades of War Resistance.* New York: WRL, 1942.

Hunt, Gaillard, ed. *Journals of the Continental Congress.* Washington, D.C.: GPO, 1910.

Kellogg, Walter. *The Conscientious Objector.* New York: Boni and Livewright, 1919.

King, Martin Luther, Jr. "Letter from a Birmingham Jail." Reprinted in Staughton Lynd, *Nonviolence in America.*

Kurland, Philip B., and Gerhard Casper. *Landmark Briefs and Arguments of the Supreme Court of the United States: Constitutional Law.* Arlington, Virginia: University Publications of America, Inc., 1975.

LaFore, Laurence. *The End of Glory: An Interpretation of the Origins of World War II.* Philadelphia: J. B. Lippincott, 1970.

Lakey, George. *Nonviolent Action, How it Works.* Wallingford, Penn.: Pendle Hill, 1963.

———. *Strategy for Nonviolent Revolution.* London: Housmans, 1970.

Larson, Zelle A. "An Unbroken Witness: Conscientious Objection to War, 1948–1953." Doctoral Dissertation, University of Hawaii, 1975.

LeFeber, Walter. *America, Russia and the Cold War: 1945–1975.* New York: Wiley, 1980.

Levy, Howard, and David Miller. *Going to Jail.* New York: Grove Press, 1970.

Lynd, Alice, ed. *We Won't Go.* Boston: Beacon Press, 1968.

Lynd, Staughton. *Nonviolence in America: A Documentary History.* Indianapolis: Bobbs-Merrill, 1966.

Lynn, Conrad. *How to Stay Out of the Army: A Guide to Your Rights Under the Draft Law.* New York: Monthly Review Press, 1968.

Mabee, Carleton. *Black Freedom: The Nonviolent Abolitionists from 1830 Through the Civil War.* New York: Macmillan, 1970.

McCague, James. *The Second Rebellion: The Story of the New York City Draft Riots of 1863.* New York: Dial Press, 1968.

Macmaster, Richard, Samual Horst, and Robert Ulle. *Conscience in Crisis: Mennonites and Other Peace Churches in America, 1739–1789; Interpretation and Documents.* Scottdale, Penn.: Herald Press, 1970.

Malbin, Michael. "Conscription, the Constitution and the Framers, An Historical Analysis." 40 *Fordham L.R.* 805 (1972).

May, Samuel. *Some Recollections of Our Anti-Slavery Conflict.* Boston: Fields, Osgood and Co., 1869.

———. *The Fugitive Slave Law and Its Victims.* Boston Public Library special collection, 1856.

Merklin, Lewis. *Those Chose Honor: The Problem of Conscience in Custody.* New York: Harper and Row, 1974.

Meyer, Ernest L. *"Hey Yellowbacks!."* New York: John Day Co., 1930.

Michel, Henri. *The Shadow War: Resistance in Europe 1939–1945.* New York: Harper and Row, 1972.

Military Manpower Task Force. *A Report to the President on Selective Service Registration.* Washington, D.C.: GPO, 1981.

Miller, Melissa, and Philip Shenk. *The Path of Most Resistance.* Scottdale, Penn.: Herald Press, 1982.

Muste, Abraham J. *Non-Violence in an Aggressive World.* New York: Harper, 1972.

————. *Not by Might: Christianity, the Way to Human Decency.* New York: Harper, 1947.

————. *Of Holy Disobedience.* Wallingford, Penn.: Pendle Hill, 1952.

————. *War Is the Enemy.* Wallingford, Penn.: Pendle Hill, 1942.

Naeve, Lowell. *A Field of Broken Stones.* Glen Gardens, N.J.: Libertarian Press, 1950.

National Security Council. *Memorandum No. 68* 1950. Cited in *Counterspy* (Washington, D.C.). Undated reprint.

Peacemakers. *Pacifists and the Korean Crisis.* SPC, 1950.

Peck, Harry. "Selective Service: Right to Counsel, Due Process, and the First Amendment." 51 *Marquette L.R.* 407 (1968).

Peck, James. *Underdogs vs. Upperdogs.* New York: AMP and R Publishers, 1980.

————. *We Who Would Not Kill.* New York: Lyle Stuart, 1958.

Penn, William. *The Rise and Progress of the Quakers.* London, 1664. University of Pennsylvania special collection.

The Pentagon Papers: The Defense Department History of United States Decision-making on Vietnam. The Senator Gravel Edition. Boston: Beacon Press, 1971–1972.

Perry, Richard, and John Cooper, eds. *Sources of Our Liberty: Documentary Origins of Individual Liberty in the United States Constitution and the Bill of Rights.* Washington, D.C.: ABA, 1952.

Pound, Roscoe. "Law in Books and Law in Action." *American Law Review Bimonthly* 44, 1. St. Louis: Review Publishing Co., 1910.

Puscheck, Herbert. "Selective Service Registration: Success or Failure." *Armed Forces and Society* (Fall 1983).

Randall, James G. *Constitutional Problems Under Lincoln.* Urbana: University of Illinois Press, 1951.

Report of the Committee of Merchants for the Relief of Colored People Suffering from the Late Riots in the City of New York. New York: George A. Whiteboine, 1863.

Rings, Werner. *Life with the Enemy: Collaboration and Resistance in Hitler's Europe 1939–1945.* New York: Doubleday, 1982.

Rivers, John C., ed. *Annals of Congress: Abridgment of the Debates of Congress from 1789 to 1856.* New York: D. Appleton and Co., 1858.

Russell, R. R. "Development of Conscientious Objection Recognition in the United States." 20 *Geo. Wash L.R.* 409 (1951–1952).

Saunders, William L., ed. *The Colonial Records of North Carolina, 1662–1776.* Raleigh, N.C.: P. M. Hale, state printer, 1886–1890.

Schlissel, Lillian, ed. *Conscience in America.* New York: Dutton, 1968.

Schroeder, John H. *Mr. Polk's War: American Opposition and Dissent, 1846–1848.* Madison: University of Wisconsin Press, 1973.

Schwartz, Bernard. *The Bill of Rights: A Documentary History.* Vol. 2. New York: Chelsea House Publishers, 1971.

———. *The Great Rights of Mankind.* New York: Oxford University Press, 1977.

Secretary of War. *Statement Concerning the Treatment of Conscientious Objectors in the Army.* Washington, D.C.: GPO, 1919.

Seeley, Robert, ed. *Handbook for Conscientious Objectors.* Philadelphia: Central Committee for Conscientious Objectors, 1982.

Semiannual Report of the Director of Selective Service. Washington, D.C.: GPO, March 1984.

Sharp, Arthur G. "Men of Peace." *Civil War Times.* (June 1982).

Sharp, Gene. *Exploring Nonviolent Alternatives.* Boston: P. Sargent, 1970.

———. *The Politics of Nonviolent Action.* Boston: P. Sargent, 1973.

Sharpless, Isaac. *A Quaker Experiment in Government.* Philadelphia: A. J. Ferris, 1898.

Shirer, William L. *The Rise and Fall of the Third Reich: A History of Nazi Germany.* N.Y.: Fawcett Crest, 1950.

Sibley, Mulford Q. *The Obligation to Disobey: Conscience and the Law.* New York: Council on Religious and International Affairs, 1970.

———. *The Political Theories of Modern Pacifism.* Philadelphia: Pacifist Research Bureau, 1944.

———. *The Quiet Battle: Writings on the Theory and Practice of Nonviolent Resistance.* Garden City, N.J.: Doubleday, 1963.

Sibley, Mulford Q., and Philip Jacob. *Conscription of Conscience: The American State and the Conscientious Objector, 1940–1947.* Ithaca, N.Y.: Cornell University Press, 1952.

Simons, H. Austin. *The Second Strike at Ft. Leavenworth.* ACLU, 1919.

Society of Shakers. *A Declaration of the Society and People (Commonly Called Shakers).* Hartford, Conn.: Hudson and Goodwin, 1815.

Stone, I. F. *The Hidden History of the Korean War*. New York: Monthly Review Press, 1969.

Stiehm, Judith. *Nonviolent Power*. Lexington, Mass.: Heath, 1972.

Sweeny, Gail White. "Conscientious Objection and the First Amendment." 14 *Akron L.R.* 71 (1980).

Taney, Roger B. "Thoughts on the Conscription Law of the United States—Rough Draft Requiring Revision." *Tylers Quarterly Historical and Genealogical Magazine* 18, 12 (October 1936).

Tanner, Edwin P. *The Province of West New Jersey, 1664–1738*. New York: Columbia University-Longmans, Green and Co. agents, 1908.

Tatum, Arlo, ed. *Handbook for Conscientious Objectors*. Philadelphia, Pennsylvania: CCCO, 1970.

Thomas, Norman. *Is Conscience a Crime?* New York: Vanguard, 1927.

Thoreau, Henry David. *On the Duty of Civil Disobedience*. Garden City, N.Y.: Doubleday, 1970.

Tolstoy's Writings on Civil Disobedience and Non-Violence. New York: Bergman Publishers, 1967.

Truman, Harry S. "Pardon Proclamation." *Federal Register* (Washington, D.C.) December 24, 1947.

Turnage, Thomas K. *Testimony Before the Subcommittee on HUD-Independent Agencies of the House Appropriations Committee*. Washington, D.C.: GPO, 1975.

Union for National Draft Opposition (UNDO). *I Say No*. N.p.: UNDO, 1970.

U.S. Bureau of Census. *Historical Statistics of the United States*. Washington, D.C.: GPO, 1975.

U.S. Bureau of Prisons. *Annual Reports*. Washington, D.C.: GPO, 1949–1977.

U.S. House of Representatives, Committee on the Judiciary, Subcommittee on Courts, Civil Liberties, and the Administration of Justice. *Amnesty Hearings*. Washington, D.C.: GPO, 1974.

———. *Implications of Draft Registration*. Washington, D.C.: GPO, 1980.

———. *Selective Service Prosecutions Hearings*. Washington, D.C.: GPO, 1982.

U.S. National Advisory Commission on Selective Service. *In Pursuit of Equity: Who Serves When Not All Serve?* Washington, D.C.: GPO, 1967.

U.S. Selective Service System. *Annual Reports*. Washington, D.C.: GPO, 1949–1976.

———. *Conscientious Objectors Special Monograph No. 11*. Washington, D.C.: GPO, 1950.

———. *Enforcement of the Selective Service Law Special Monograph No. 14*. Washington, D.C.: GPO, 1950.

Useem, Michael. *Conscription, Protest, and Social Change*. New York: Wiley, 1973.

Villard, Fanny G. *William L. Garrison on Non-Resistance*. New York: Haskell House, 1973.

Vipont, Elfrida. *The Story of Quakerism*. Richmond, Indiana: Friends United Press, 1954.

Waters, Frank. *Book of the Hopi*. N.Y.: Ballantine, 1963.

Weber, David. *Civil Disobedience in America*. Ithaca, N.Y.: Cornell University Press, 1978.

Webster, Daniel. "Conscription Speech to the House of Representatives," December 9, 1814. Reprinted in *Congressional Record*, July 7, 1970.

White, James. "Processing Conscientious Objector Claims: A Constitutional Inquiry." 56 *Calif. L.R.* 652 (1968).

Why We Refused to Register. SPC, 1940.

Wittner, Lawrence S. *Rebels Against War: The American Peace Movement, 1941–1960*. New York: Columbia University Press, 1969.

Zahn, Gordon C. *War, Conscience, and Dissent*. New York: Hawthorn Books, 1967.

Zimmer, Timothy. *Letters of a Conscientious Objector*. Valley Forge, Penn.: Judson Press, 1969.

Zinn, Howard. *A People's History of the United States*. New York: Harper and Row, 1980.

Index

Index

163

About the Author

STEPHEN M. KOHN is the Clinical Director of the Government Accountability Project and an Adjunct Professor of Law at the Antioch School of Law. A former National Endowment for the Humanities Youthgrants Fellow, he has written extensively on peace and constitutional law and is currently working on a book concerning Sedition Act prosecutions in the United States.

About the Author